Th[...]

GIANCARLO
GIAMBRONE

THE GOLDEN AGE

The impact of the 50's on America

LUCCA
Extra Virgin Olive Oil

Product of Italy

3 L (3 qt 5.4 fl oz)

By Joe Reina
author of
The Goat Sleeps in The Kitchen,
Italy Under My Skin,
Giancarlo Giambrone

ISBN 979-8-89309-773-3 (Paperback)
ISBN 979-8-89309-775-7 (Hardcover)
ISBN 979-8-89309-774-0 (Digital)

Covenant Books
11661 Hwy 707
Murrells Inlet, SC 29576
www.covenantbooks.com

Giancarlo, February 1950

To Kelly Reina Schuster and Michael J. Reina

ACKNOWLEDGMENTS

My heartfelt Thanks to Patricia Benesh of AuthorsAssist.com for her help in bringing my thoughts to fruition. She has been there constantly from day one at my beck and call. To Kelly Reina Schuster for her time in proofreading, and certainly credit is due to Michelle Holmes and the editing crew at covenant books.

My sincere gratitude to Jim Parkhurst of Parkhurst Artworks for his creation of the title page artwork, and with the photos.

INTRODUCTION

What was it like in America to live in the 1950s? The US was recovering from World War II, and Americans were ready to move on to a new era, a new age.

This is the story of a man facing the 1950s. You may have read *Giancarlo Giambrone: The Life and Times of One of the World's Great Financial Minds*, my previous novel. In this sequel, Giancarlo is a successful businessman, presumably retired but intrigued by the changing cultural landscape of the 1950s. Not since the roaring '20s had the US experienced such a dominant change in its culture, economy, music, literature, and all forms of entertainment, the most important being television.

In 1950, only 4,500 homes had TV. By the end of the decade, forty-five million of American households had one. It became a family thing, to the extent the family would eat dinner watching it.

The boom in the economy that began right after World War II continued even stronger. Some women who worked during the war returned to the kitchen to care for the family and resumed the responsibilities for weekend entertainment, barbecues, picnics, sport activities, and travel. Others chose to remain in the workforce, establishing a greater female presence.

Leisure time was ever present. People began playing tennis, golf, and bowling, and apparel for specific sports became popular.

Suburban housing developments were booming. People moved to the suburbs in droves, which prompted developers to build shopping centers and the government to build schools and roads.

Automobiles were the highlight of transportation. Soon, there were *classics* like the European sports cars that inspired General Motors to introduce the Corvette and Ford to launch the Thunderbird, coveted by collectors today.

With nonstop flights, larger airplanes enabled an increase in the number of passengers with reduced fares, so more people could afford to travel. This increased hotel development and restaurants, which enhanced the economy, creating a new category of business.

Movies changed and became open to sex, as did magazines such as *Playboy*. Stars like Marilyn Monroe, Jane Russell, James Dean, and Marlon Brando brought a rebellious approach to the scene. The Legion of Decency, founded in 1932, a Catholic-backed organization that initially was to watch over language and sex in movies, lost its power over Hollywood. It no longer was a factor in control of the industry. Frank Sinatra, who was down-and-out in the early '50s, made a glorious comeback in the movie adaptation of James Jones's bestseller *From Here to Eternity*, which was about WWII. It was initially banned by the legion, was released, and Sinatra won an Academy Award for his role. He earned $8,000 for that role.

Music was in a major upheaval. Black entertainers and musicians, historically segregated, were accepted by whites, especially among young Americans. Rock and roll was embraced by both whites and blacks. It became the crossover of both white and black singers and musicians. Bill Haley and his band recorded "Rock around the Clock," and it dominated all the radio stations, as was the case with black singer Little Richard and his rendition of "Tutti Frutti." This launched a new era in music. The first major black recording studio, commonly referred to as Motown in Detroit, was established, and the top black musicians and singers finally got the recognition they deserved.

The Civil Rights Movement was sparked by a brave woman named Rosa Parks, who refused to give up her seat on a bus in Montgomery, Alabama. The bus driver had her arrested, which fueled protests across the South. Martin Luther King led the protests and later established his church, the Ebenezer Baptist Church.

The movement really began in 1947, when the Brooklyn Dodgers signed the first black baseball player, Jackie Robinson, and opened the door for blacks in all professional sports. It was the beginning of lifting the dark cloud of segregation in America, but it was a slow process.

A major concern surfaced when Russia launched the Sputnik space capsule. It created a greater rift between the US and the powerful Russian government. Thus, the Cold War became of great concern because of the possibility of a nuclear war. It was ever present on the minds of all Americans, so much so that grade-school children were trained on what to do in the event of a bomb alert.

In this novel, Giancarlo experiences the throes and thrills of these changes firsthand and navigates some new business challenges in this new era, later deemed the golden age.

CHAPTER 1

Lucca, Italy
July 1950

I strolled out to the balcony of our recently renovated villa in Tuscany with a glass of wine to catch one last glance of the three hundred acres of olive groves we owned. I marveled at the maze of two-hundred-year-old olive trees planted by my family. These groves had survived droughts and historical havoc at times, including wars and political upheaval.

The grove and the olive oil business passed through the generations in our family with no serious problems. The business seemed to run by itself, given Giuseppe Fragale, the third-generation caretaker in charge of operation, who handled it so well. I was very lucky to have him.

It had been two months since we celebrated my fiftieth birthday in the south of France, a weekend forever indelible in my mind. Gina, my lovely wife, covered all the bases. It was not to be forgotten. Recently, she sensed I was getting bored and surprised me with plane tickets and arrangements for our journey to our other villa in Siracusa, Sicily.

As I sipped my wine, I heard footsteps, and Gina joined me on the balcony. She put her arms around me, gave me a kiss on the cheek, and said, "Giancarlo, I bet I can guess what you're thinking. While you're excited to get back to our great house in Siracusa, you hate to leave Lucca, knowing we will not be back for a year."

"As is always the case, my mind-reading sweetheart, you are correct."

The sun was about to set in the cloudless blue sky, and Gina took the wineglass from my hand and finished it. We watched the sun go down. Not a word was exchanged; our minds were blank. It seemed like the sun was not in a hurry to set completely.

Gina looked at me with those big brown eyes and said, "Let's go, handsome. I have some plans for you tonight, and they do not include dancing."

I was sad to leave Lucca as we drove through the hills of Tuscany the next morning to Firenze. The natural beauty never ceases to amaze me. We flew to Catania, Sicily, and our caretaker Vincenzo picked us up. In less than eight hours, we arrived at our Shangri-la in Siracusa. In the past, we'd travel by train to Rome, by sea to Agrigento, then by auto to Siracusa, normally a grueling eighteen hours. This trip by air was a joy compared to the past.

At 6:00 p.m., I was ushered out to our patio with a glass of Chianti. Gina and Alena, our chef and housekeeper, began what I was told would be a surprise feast.

It was another bright day without a cloud in the sky. For a moment, I just stared at the sea then looked up and thanked God for my blessings—my journey that brought us here: ten years as a successful stockbroker in New York in the wild '20s, six years as a banker in Chicago in the '30s, and the real money as a real-estate developer after World War II. Two villas in Italy topped with a beautiful home in Palm Springs. And then there was Gina.

I am a firm believer there is no such thing as coincidence. Every day a page turns for us in that book in the sky. Some days, nothing significant happens, and then like a thunderbolt, we get hit with something that changes our lives. That thunderbolt for me happened in Washington, DC, when I met Gina. I was like a kid in a candy store. It took all but two minutes for me to fall in love with her, and every day since is like sticking my hands—not hand—in the cookie jar. Turn the word *love* over and on the other side, it reads, "Gina."

She has it all. She's bright, a great personality, great looks, and a figure to go with them. The best part about her personality is her quick wit. I felt grateful to have her by my side.

I sat down and opened my latest book, *The Fountainhead* by Ayn Rand. It was her first book. I had read about her struggles in getting it published. A dozen firms refused to publish it, then the early critics failed to give it a high rating. But once it got high praise by the *New York Times*, it sold more than eight million copies, and the young Russian author received the fame she so well deserved.

I felt my stomach rumble, and a short time later, the smells wafting from the kitchen left no doubt in my mind as to the surprise. Gina strolled out with a platter of meatballs that sent me back to my youth.

I am reminded of the times I sat in this same chair with my dad and my mom serving us this same appertivo, cherished memories filled with warmth and love, this brings a smile to my face and a sense of peace to my heart. The thoughts of my parents, always present when we are here, brought tears to my eyes. Gina asked, "So, Giancarlo, what are your thoughts right now?"

"I can't tell you how many times I sat in this very chair as a young teenager and savored the same meatballs served by my mother to me and my dad. There are so many memories of my childhood summers here on this patio. Thank you, Gina, for evoking them.

My father had laid out my future as I approached graduation from secondary school. There was no choice—first two years of university at his alma mater, U of Bologna, then two years at his second alma mater, Princeton. My respect for him was such that I went along with the program, and I am so happy I did. It led to the path for my business success both as a stockbroker and a banker."

Gina smiled. "Excuse me, Giancarlo, don't you want to add something? What am I, a walk on?"

As always with her, she loved to needle me.

She continued, "I have a few trips planned for you, my love. I know boredom has begun to creep into your life. I know how much you love to read, but I want to see more of this great part of the world with you while we are here over the next three months. I want to visit Ragusa."

"Sounds good, Gina. I like the idea of a few side trips, but I want to go into town and buy a TV for the house first thing in the morning. I miss what's happening in the world. I'm very concerned about the war in Korea and afraid President Truman is going to get our country into a war in Vietnam. The war hawks in the military, and some of those in Congress are pressuring him to provide more aid to the French fighting there. They are using scare tactics, that if the North Vietnamese succeed, there could be a threat of communism spreading throughout Asia."

"Giancarlo, please don't get yourself all wound up in something we have no control over. We are in Paradiso and about to eat your favorite, *pasta e polpette*."

"Hmm, I love when you speak Italian. Perhaps we should go upstairs and have dessert and delay dinner for a while."

"Be nice, wild man. Alena spent all morning hand making the pasta, and we should be eating in a few minutes."

"I am looking forward to our feast. Tomorrow morning, we'll purchase the TV before we head to Ragusa."

The next morning, after a two-hour drive to Ragusa, we arrived in the city center in time for lunch. We stumbled into what turned out to be one of the oldest restaurants in town, Taberna Dei Cinque Sensi. Gina's Italian conversation warmed the old gentleman who seated us. She said to him, "Forget the menu. Feed us."

He laughed and looked at me as if to say, "You are one lucky guy to have her on your arm. I can only imagine what it must be like to wake up next to her every morning."

I smiled ever so slightly.

We ate like kings, shared a cannoli, and later strolled the town. Walking in this ancient city that had not been subjected to the ravages of World War II seemed like time had stood still for two thousand years.

We dined in a small trattoria where the food would stand up to any fine restaurant in any major city in the world. The town was so clean, it seemed like a crew would come in every morning and sweep the streets and manicure the plants. Our walk highlighted the day, complimented by the sun and the cloudless sky. I thought about the old gentleman in the restaurant. He was right. I am the luckiest man alive to have Gina by my side, and I thanked her for the suggestion to visit Ragusa.

Siracusa
October 1950

The summer in Siracusa was like a blur, and Gina was anxious to get back to Palm Springs. The memory of that horrible November crossing the Atlantic never left her. It was a disastrous, rough ocean voyage in 1948, and Gina spent a good deal of it in bed with seasickness. She began plans for the trip back to Los Angeles.

For me, it was always sad to leave Siracusa. The memories of Mom and Dad were there almost daily. Then the food—nowhere in the world were the fruit and vegetables any better, picked ripe off the vines and trees. Same for the fish—Alena and Gina shopped at the fish market, and while the fish were not flopping around, they were still alive. We never ate anything that had been frozen or processed. Alena never bought a loaf of bread in her life; she learned to make bread and pasta at the age of ten. For some reason, she never married.

We were very fortunate to have great staff at both Italian villas, Giuseppe in Lucca to look after the olive oil business and Anna to care for the house and cook the great meals we shared. We were blessed with Alena filling that role here and Vincenzo Gallo our caretaker looking after the house and the gardens in Siracusa.

Having finished *The Fountainhead*, I purchased two books for the trip, Hemingway's *Across the River and into the Trees* and Mika Waltari's *The Egyptian*, both *New York Times* bestsellers. I was eager to read them on the journey to Palm Springs. Vincenzo drove us to Agrigento, and as always, the glistening sun on the Mediterranean was delightful. I lost count as to how many times we made that trip.

"Giancarlo, I know how sad you are leaving our haven in Siracusa. Soon, we will be with the Venegonis and the Bomarittos, our friends in Palm Springs, and savoring some great dinners and enjoying time with them, something we miss by not having those kinds of friends here in Italy. And with the new books you have, we will be in Palm Springs before you know it. So please cheer up."

Our relationship with Tom and Sandra Venegoni dated back to my early days as a stock broker in the '20s, and we treasured the friendship. The same feelings existed for Sharon and Tony Bomaritto, friends from our country club.

"Come here, sweetheart. Let me give you a hug. You always have that sixth sense of knowing where my head is. I'll be fine. I just wish there was a way to wiggle my nose and be there."

*****

Palm Springs
October 1950

The two-week trip across the Atlantic was flawless, not a single incident, as was the flight to Los Angeles. Tom and Sandra greeted us warmly at the airport, and we drove to our home in Palm Springs. They had stocked our home with food and back issues of the *Los Angeles Times* that we missed while on our trip. Tom said, "Hey, you two, I bought some new records for you, two new hot black singers, both from St. Louis—Chuck Berry and a husband-wife team called Ike and Tina Turner. Let me put them on the record player."

As we listened to the music, Gina piped up and said, "Let's go to Lord Fletcher's for dinner."

When we arrived at Fletcher's, we saw Frank Sinatra in his favorite booth with Ava Gardner. Both Gina and Sandra were mesmerized by Sinatra, and Tom and I couldn't take our eyes off Ava Gardner.

For our meal, we had the usual chicken and dumplings, their signature dish, and shared a bottle of Gavi di Gavi and headed home. Jet lag caught up with us, and we called it a night. An interesting thing to note: the restaurant was jammed, yet no one bothered Sinatra and his lady.

Tom and I were on the golf course early the next morning. We both commented on Ava Gardner. Tom said, "Giancarlo, do you think they will marry?"

"Well, Tom, Sinatra has hit rock bottom. I recently read he is in dire straits. His records aren't selling, he owes money for back taxes, and he is in debt to the banks. Yet her career is flourishing. So I don't know how long she'll stay with him. She is notorious for leaving men at the drop of a hat. I wouldn't wager on this relationship lasting."

Later that afternoon, Gina and I began reading the newspaper editions of the past ten days. We both marveled at the changes that were impacting the country. This was especially true in the new books that appeared on the best-selling list, which included *Return to Paradise* by James Michener and *From Here to Eternity* by James Jones. The music critics were especially favorable with their praise for Nat King Cole's records of "Mona Lisa" and "Too Young," along with Ivory Joe Hunter's "I Almost Lost My Mind." Included in the group was "I Wanna be Loved" by Dinah Washington.

For the most part, except for Nat King Cole, we had never heard of these people. We found this rise in popularity somewhat surprising. Black singers were becoming part of the mainstream in music. American books and entertainment were changing too.

Meanwhile, I was still concerned about the war. As always, Gina sensed my mood. "Giancarlo, let's go see a movie. I want to see *The African Queen* with Humphrey Bogart and Katharine Hepburn."

"You mean you want me to turn off the TV so that I avoid concern about us entering another war."

"Yes, come on. Throw on a pair of trousers. We can make the 7:00 p.m. show if we hurry."

A newsreel was shown about the war in Korea, and for the first time, Gina showed interest. The movie did take my mind off of the news for a while.

The ensuing weeks went by quickly, and we made plans to spend the holidays with Sandra and Tom as our guests. We booked a table with them and Tony and Sharon for New Year's Eve at the country club. We brought in 1951 quietly. I was wondering if books and movies would be enough to occupy my mind in the new year.

Gina Giambrone

CHAPTER 2

January 1951

January was exceptionally cool, and Tom and I were unable to play golf. It gave me time to read and reflect on my current life in retirement. Gina had purchased a book about Napoleon's fiancée, *Désirée*, by Annemarie Selinku, which I was about to start.

On January 19, we received a cable from Anna in Lucca. It ultimately altered our lives. The cable read,

> Giancarlo I am very sorry to report,
> Giuseppe our caretaker has had a heart attack
> and died. Please come back, we are sad and des-
> perate, we do not know what to do.

The shock left Gina and me speechless. "Gina, Giuseppe has been caring for the olive oil business and the olive groves for the past thirty years, as did his father and grandfather before him."

"What will you do, Giancarlo? Will you sell the business?"

"Come on, Gina. That business has been in my family for two centuries. There's no way I can sell it."

"Well, why don't you take charge and hire someone to run the day-to-day operation and get involved in marketing the olive oil?"

"That sounds like the only way to proceed, Gina. Perhaps my retirement days were over."

We made plans to fly to New York, using Pan Am Airways to Rome, with a connecting flight to Firenze. Tom and Sandra drove us to Los Angeles Airport for our flight to New York. There was dead silence. Gina and I were still in shock over the death of Giuseppe. My mind was racing over the decisions I needed to make. Gina's hand never left mine. She stayed calm after we received the news, which helped me remain calm.

The trip to Rome was without incident. It took fifteen hours. We flew from Rome, after a four-hour layover, to Firenze. There, we hired a driver to take us to Lucca. With the time difference, we had been traveling for thirty-six hours. Fortunately, we got a little sleep on the trip across the Atlantic, but we were exhausted when we finally arrived at our villa. Anna greeted us in tears, and I had everything I could do to hold back my emotion, but Gina broke down and cried.

We had a snack and went to bed, but sleep and jet lag kept me awake through most of the night, and anxiety caught up with me. I went to the kitchen, seeking a cup of coffee, knowing Anna was already making the day's bread.

My first thought was to make arrangements with the funeral director in town to bury Giuseppe. Since he had no family, we opted not to have a wake. We had a simple ceremony at the cemetery, with Anna and the olive oil employees. We laid Giuseppe to rest, went home, and had lunch with those who attended the burial. The priest joined us for lunch.

After the priest read the normal prayers, he spoke for a few moments and paid tribute to Giuseppe. "He was a good Catholic. Do not think of Giuseppe with tears. He would not want you to be sad. Think of him laughing as he did so many times when you celebrated the great feasts at harvest time and those after pressing the oil over the years."

Indeed, Giuseppe would be greatly missed.

The next day, I went to town and spoke to a few friends searching someone to replace Giuseppe, but it was fruitless. I returned in time to have lunch with Gina and voiced my concern about finding a replacement.

9

Anna overheard part of the conversation. "Excuse me, Giancarlo, but if I may suggest, Giuseppe relied heavily on his assistant Salvatore Vitale for almost everything, including harvesting the olives in the fall and pressing them to make the oil. Why don't you speak to him and see if he is interested in taking on the responsibility?"

Gina's smile could light up a Christmas tree, and my mouth dropped. I got up from my chair and hugged Anna. She was shocked. I had always refrained from showing any emotion with her out of respect for the employee-owner relationship, to say nothing of her never showing any emotion about anything until the death of Giuseppe.

After lunch, I went out to the field and found Salvatore and invited him to the house. We discussed the opportunity and salary, and he graciously accepted my offer. He was married with a young child and had a brother living in Lucca. Both were from Sicily.

While he knew the day-to-day operation, he knew little about marketing the oil and, of course, knew none of the clients. Gina and I had a long discussion on the subject of marketing the oil, and she finally said, "Giancarlo, you have been bored. Perhaps it was too early to retire. Are you ready to step in and take on that part of the business? Before you answer, realize it will alter our lifestyle."

"I was thinking that Gina. Both your statements have crossed my mind since we received the news of Giuseppe's death. Perhaps I can get involved and find a person to train and ultimately take over. That was the case with the bank when I hired Jimmy Boscamp.

As to our lifestyle, the current business is all here in Italy, none in Sicily, and none in the US. So we'll spend the same time here in Italy, six months in developing the business and, as in the past, live the rest of the year in America, where I can introduce our olive oil to the US and possibly Canada, maybe even South America."

"Oh, boy, Giancarlo, I knew I should have never suggested you take over the marketing. There goes our lifestyle."

I grabbed her, threw my arms around her, kissed her, and said, "Do you have any idea how excited I am about this challenge?"

"Mr. Giambrone, do you have any idea how happy I am for you?"

I needed to learn the olive oil business. My early plans were to call on our Italian distributors that were scattered throughout Italy. I drove to Milan with two goals: first to visit the economic development commission to see if there was any possible financial help exporting olive oil to the US. I met with two gentlemen from the financial division and was told there was no aid for exporting any product to the US.

Next I called on our distributor for the Lombardy Region, Don Giovanni Ruggeri and Sons. During our very formal meeting, I learned they had not seen anyone from our firm in years, and they greeted me coldly. I asked them about the business, and they said it was slow, but part of the problem was price. It was too expensive to use for cooking. Italians cooked with lard. I made a mental note to discuss this with Anna upon my return.

I came away from that meeting somewhat disgruntled, but on the drive home, I reached back to the early days of banking during the depression and remembered the things we did to attract customers to our bank. Free coffee every morning and occasional soups at lunchtime in the bank cafeteria—and not to forget offering a half point more interest on savings accounts than other banks in town. We also hired two salesmen to call on businesses, offering more competitive terms than competitive banks. I decided to use that experience to create incentives for distributors, purveyors, and restaurants to buy our olive oil.

Gina and I had lunch on the balcony when I returned, and we discussed my trip. When Anna began serving, I asked her if she cooked with lard, and she replied yes. "But, Anna, why? We have plenty of olive oil."

"Pardon me, Giancarlo, I always cooked like my mother did. Olive oil was too expensive."

"Thank you, Anna, but please, from now on, cook with olive oil. It is healthier than lard."

And the light bulb went off. I saw that Gina sensed it that very moment. "Giancarlo, there's the clue. Increase the volume, get the price down, and promote the fact that olive oil is healthier. Sell the olive oil on the strength of that message."

"I have another idea, Gina. What about other uses for it. Next time I am in Milan, I am going to engage some scientists to begin studying other options for its use."

Siracusa
July

We flew from Firenze to Catania for our return to Siracusa. Vincenzo picked us up, and we took the pleasant drive along the sea to our villa. Alena was ready for us as always when we arrived. We went upstairs to refresh and returned to the kitchen to see what she had planned for lunch. She scooted us out to the patio with a glass of wine to relax before lunch.

Soon, she showed up with ravioli in a sage-and-butter sauce, which was to die for. I asked her to bring a small bowl with olive oil so we could dip our warm bread. She smiled and soon returned with my request. Olive oil for dipping our bread—another first.

When we finished lunch, she came to clean the table and later brought tiramisu for dessert. I asked, "Alena, do you cook with lard?"

I received the same answer Anna had given. She replied, "Yes. It was the way I learned to cook."

I asked her to begin cooking with olive oil. A look crossed her face, as if to say that is insane. "But, Giancarlo, it is too expensive."

"Alena, I will have Salvatore send you a year's supply. Do not be concerned about the cost. Please immediately begin to cook with olive oil. Gina and I will be shopping tomorrow, and we'll buy some good oil for you."

The next morning, Gina and I went into town. We stopped at a café for a cappuccino and discussed plans for our stay. "Gina, I want to take some trips while we are here to explore the business. We do not have a distributor in Sicily, and it's a big market. It'll be fun because we can explore the countryside as we did in Ragusa."

"Okay, Giancarlo, but please let us have a life. Let's not allow the olive oil business to consume our lives as the real-estate-development business did in the '40s after the war."

"I'm with you. That's why I said we can combine the trips with pleasure as we did when we were in Ragusa."

A few days later, we departed for our first trip to Agrigento, a seaport city that attracted many tourists and, for that reason, had many restaurants. We met the restaurant owners, first introducing ourselves, and then inquired about what they cooked with, and we always received the same answers—*lard*. When I asked why not olive oil, the replies were again the same; it was too expensive. I suggested, why not put a small dish on the table with olive oil so people could dip their bread in it, and they laughed at me.

Our next stop was Marsala, also on the sea. We did the same, spent two nights, and again received the same negative news in the restaurants. We were told olive oil was used primarily for salads. I asked the owners who they were buying their oil from, and the question was ignored. All I received was a negative shake of their heads.

We next traveled to Palermo, the capital of Sicily, and we were told, "We fry with lard."

I received the same answers to my questions about their suppliers. However, in one of the smaller restaurants, when I inquired about the provider, I got a simple answer, "Signore, you don't want to know."

I changed the subject and talked to the owner when Gina went to the washroom. I explained it was her birthday, and I wanted something special for our meal. He winked and said, "Let me speak to my wife, the chef, and I promise it will be a meal and birthday she will never forget."

And that it was! We were served Cornish hen, deboned, with a sauce that was so good, we could not stop dipping our bread in it. Observing this, the owner brought a small bowl of it to us. And the best was dessert, a small chocolate cake with a candle.

After dinner, Gina put her arms around me and said, "Handsome, you surprised me. I thought for sure you had forgotten my birthday. You get your award when we get back to the hotel, sweetheart. You dodged a bullet with this dinner. Tell the truth. Had you forgotten it?"

I just smiled. My mind shifted to our return to the hotel.

When we returned to our car, Gina looked at me and said, "Why did he say you don't want to know who sells him his olive oil?"

"Because, my dear inquisitive wife, he is buying it from a Mafia-controlled vendor. They probably control the entire business, which includes the olive groves, processing the oil and marketing it with their distributors throughout the entire island."

"Giancarlo, I am frightened about this. Please promise me you will not pursue doing business in Sicily."

*****

September

I decided to honor both Gina's requests, avoiding the business in Sicily and, more emphatically, never allowing the business to overtake our lives. It was time to relax in Siracusa for the remaining weeks of our stay. I wanted to read, listen to music, watch a little TV, and pay attention to Gina.

We spent the next few days shopping for recordings of some of the new and classic singers, which included Nat King Cole's new release "Unforgettable," Tony Bennett's "Because of You," Dinah Washington's latest "I Won't Cry Anymore," and Little Richard's insane "Tutti Frutti."

At the bookstore, I bought *The Robe* by Lloyd Douglas, which is about the Roman tribune who had captured Jesus's robe after the crucifixion. He wore it for a while and later had a nervous breakdown. After he recovered, he traveled back to Judea with a strong desire to learn about Jesus. It was a powerful book.

Our pleasure was always compromised by the bad news with the war in Korea. North Korea and the Chinese Army had suffered five hundred thousand deaths and casualties, and they continued to fight on, and American and Allied casualties and deaths were also mounting.

President Truman continued to send military aid to the French fighting in Vietnam. My concern continued to rise with it. I told Gina, "What is Truman going to do when the French have had it, as is always the case in any war? Sooner or later, they will give up, make concessions, and leave. Now his determination to support any country that is threatened with communism leaves him with no choice. It surely will get us into that war. It is ridiculous, a country with little if any natural resources, determined to achieve their independence."

"Giancarlo, I thought we were going to spend the rest of our time here relaxing and avoiding anything to interrupt it"

"You're right, Gina. I'll turn the TV off. Let's go see a movie."

We went to see *A Streetcar Named Desire.* It won an Academy Award earlier that year. Later, we saw another Academy winner, *A Place in the Sun.* Movies certainly had a welcome salubrious effect.

October

I asked Alena to cook Pasta alla Norma for our last supper. It was involved because of the eggplant and special cheeses, and she agreed. It was to be the first time she fried eggplant with olive oil. Gina and I went to the store and bought extra virgin olive oil, young eggplant, and both cheeses she requested. That evening, we opened a bottle of amarone red wine and celebrated what was the best meal of the trip.

Vincenzo drove us to Catania the next morning for our flight to Rome. I sent a cable to Tom Venegoni to see if he and Sandra could meet us and received confirmation they would pick us up and drive us to Palm Springs.

The thirty-hour trip seemed to go faster than the one coming over, perhaps because we read and slept part of it. Tom and Sandra picked us up. We were hungry, so we stopped on the way to Palm Springs at In-N-Out Burger, feasted, and continued home, happy to be there. The four of us crashed for the night.

CHAPTER 3

Palm Springs
October 1951

Gina and I woke up Sunday morning after an incredible night's sleep. The long trip, along with the nine-hour time difference, caught up with us. Sandra and Tom were already awake and had coffee brewing. Sandra was ready for breakfast with our favorite, blueberry pancakes. Tom opened the conversation, "So, Giancarlo, how was the trip?"

"Tom, we solved many problems. We put Giuseppe to rest and hired his replacement, who was his assistant. I have decided to come out of retirement to handle the marketing for the company, which will include bringing our oil to the US."

"Wow! I told Sandra you were going to do that. I am happy for you, Giancarlo. This will keep your mind active and help maintain the two-hundred-year history of your family's business."

"I want to call Tony Bomaritto and get a lunch date this week. Will you join us, Tom?"

"Of course. What's the occasion?"

"I want to get his theory about cooking with olive oil in his restaurant."

Sandra said, "Giancarlo, don't you think it's too expensive?"

"Yes, Sandra. I have been getting that response. The price of olive oil will have to come down, which I'll work on. We will have to increase our production and increase the sales volume. But like all new products, this is always the case. Look at the TV business. When the first TVs went on sale, the prices were ridiculously high. Two years ago, the average American family could not afford one.

Less than three million homes had a TV set. Today, because prices are more reasonable, ten million homes have one.

"Henry Ford was the first to realize this when he came up with the idea to mass produce the Ford Model T. He made his automobile available for everyone."

Gina, laughing, said, "Here we go. I can just see your picture on the cover of *Time* magazine, Giancarlo, with the quote, 'Giancarlo Giambrone, olive oil's answer to the Ford Model T!'"

I interrupted, "Can we eat now, Susan? It is getting a little deep here." I turned to Tom. "Tom, what do you get when you overeducate a woman?"

"I am not about to answer that, Giancarlo. And may I suggest this is a good time for you to exercise good judgment and keep your mouth shut, unless of course you intend on sleeping on the couch tonight."

"Perhaps you're right. Let's eat."

*****

Tom and I met with Tony Bomaritto on the golf course later that week. I refrained from discussing the olive oil business so we could concentrate on our game. At lunch, I brought up my idea. I prefaced cooking with it by stressing the health benefit, to say nothing about the improvement in taste. I received the same negative answer regarding the cost. I said, "Tony, do you use olive oil to cook at home?"

"As a matter of fact, we do, Giancarlo, and there's no doubt food tastes much better. Please try to understand. Food costs must be closely watched in the restaurant business, or you'll be working for the purveyors. The business will not be profitable. Get the price down and then do a selling job on the health and taste benefits, and maybe you'll have some success. But in my humble opinion, you have hard work ahead of you."

He hesitated then continued, "One other thing, Giancarlo: don't rely on the restaurant business. You have to reach the food-distribution network, along with the food purveyors that sell to the better restaurants.

"In addition, there are many fine food stores that specialize in Italian food imports, mostly in predominant Italian-Sicilian neighborhoods. They are prized potential customers. Let me make a few calls and see if I can get an audience with some of my purveyors, and I'll go with you to make the presentations. Did you bring any samples of your oil?"

"Thanks, Tony. As a matter of fact, I am expecting a shipment of samples in about ten days. Some are bottled, some in three-liter cans. Please proceed to make some contacts. Thanks for your time. Let's have lunch."

We had the Venegonis and Tony and Sharon Bomaritto join us for an early dinner. Gina cooked Pasta alla Norma, frying the eggplant in olive oil, with Sandra by her side. Then Sandra made the salad using our olive oil for the dressing. We placed a small bowl of oil on the table and passed it around so that everyone could dip their warm Italian bread.

Sharon asked Gina about the preparation for the sauce for the pasta, and Gina stressed the fact she fried the eggplant in olive oil. Tony, laughing, said, "Giancarlo, are you trying to send us a message here about the many uses of olive oil?"

I looked at Tony with a smile and sarcastically said, "Tony, whatever gave you that impression?"

Gina remained quiet in all the discussions about the olive oil business from the minute we arrived from Sicily. I quizzed her about it in bed that night. "Giancarlo, I am keeping an open mind about the business even though early on, it was my suggestion you should handle the marketing. I am just concerned that it is going to impact our incredible lifestyle. It seems to me your work is cut out for you."

"Gina, I have never walked away from hard work, and the same attitude holds true for a challenge. I met all the challenges thrown at me by the stock market. I intend to attack the olive business with the same mindset."

The next night, the six of us went to a movie, *Quo Vadis*, to see Sophia Loren, the "hot" new Italian actress' first movie. It left no doubt that we witnessed a future superstar.

Afterward, we went to the country club for a drink, and Tom brought up the subject about the Italian influence on America. "Think about how much we owe the Italians: pizza, pasta, cappuccino, risotto, parmigiana cheese, along with all the Italian cheeses, and let's not forget prosciutto and Italian bread and the great Italian wines. Sophia Loren joins Frank Sinatra, Tony Bennett, and Perry Como and all the other Italian artists."

Tony added, "Soon, Italian olive oil will be part of the mix!"

I raised my glass to that notion.

The next day, Gina and Sandra went shopping while Tom and I played golf. They returned with new record albums, which included Nat King Cole, Tony Bennett, Chuck Berry, Ella Fitzgerald, and Perry Como. "Giancarlo, I bought some new books for you: *The Old Man and the Sea* by Hemingway, *Giant* by Edna Ferber, and a third, *East of Eden*, John Steinbeck's latest."

"Thanks, Gina. You know how I want to keep up with the new authors and books. I can't wait to start on one of them. Meanwhile, what's for lunch?"

We had a nice lunch prepared with calamari fried with olive oil and a cannellini bean soup laced with olive oil. Gina's idea was to continue recipes to enhance the product. Tom and Sandra were beginning to believe.

The olive oil samples arrived, and I placed a call to Tony. He made arrangements to meet with two of his largest food purveyors in Los Angeles. I was well prepared for negative comments with incentive prices. At each meeting, after a brief introduction, we poured sample oil into a small bowl for the bread Tony brought from his restaurant. At both meetings, we received the positive "taste test" we hoped for. We got *test* orders from both the purveyors.

Tony said, "Giancarlo, you are one hell of a salesman. I am shocked, and I am going to join them as your third success for the day. I will issue a purchase order for you as soon as I get to my office.

"Giancarlo, in the cities of New York, Boston, San Francisco, St. Louis, and Chicago, there are large concentrations of Italians and Sicilians, including Little Italy neighborhoods with many Italian restaurants and specialty grocery stores that stock only Italian imports. They should be your next challenge. If I may suggest, you can't do this by yourself. You're going to need some sales help."

"Tony, thanks for all this. I appreciate your time and welcome other ideas and suggestions. Do you have any contacts in those cities?"

"I do, Giancarlo. Let me get to my office, and I'll put a list together, and I'll bring it this weekend when I come to the desert for our golf game."

*****

Back in Palm Springs, I discussed my plans with Gina. "Gina, I want to have the Bomarittos for dinner over the weekend. Tony is working on some contacts for my next trip to St. Louis and Chicago. Are you planning on going with me?"

"Of course I am joining you. I would not miss it for anything, I love watching you in action!"

"Hmm, are we thinking of the same action?"

"Calm down, butcher boy. We are trying to sell olive oil. We are not making some hot love-story movie."

Sharon and Tony arrived Saturday, and we shared a bottle of Cervaro, our favorite Italian white wine. Gina had gone to the bakery and bought a nice loaf of bread, and she took a little olive oil, mixed it with garlic and basil, and made a pesto sauce. She put it on the table with the bread brushed with olive oil she had toasted and served our guests.

Both Sharon and Tony were overwhelmed. Laughing, Sharon said, "Well, Gina, that's it. We have not had dinner yet, and I can only imagine what surprises are lurking in the kitchen, but rest assured you two will not be invited to our house for dinner anymore."

Gina laid it on thick for the main course after we shared a little pasta primavera. She made scampi sautéed with olive oil and lemon juice, along with asparagus parmigiana.

While the ladies were clearing the table, Tony and I sat down and reviewed his list of contacts in San Francisco, St. Louis, and Chicago. I made notes about them, especially his good friend in St. Louis. Ironically, that friend had the same last name—no relation—and his restaurant also was called Tony's. His name was Vince Bommarito.

"Giancarlo, my friend Tony's restaurant is much more upscale than mine when it comes to food presentation and wine selection. His is a designation restaurant. It is in the downtown section of St. Louis, and price is no object for the clients he caters to.

"When the food reaches a table, it is an artistic presentation and resembles a piece of art. People sit and stare momentarily and marvel at it. Getting a reservation is extremely difficult, unless one is a well-known client or a celebrity. A request for a table for Friday or Saturday has a two-month wait.

"His Italian wine selection rivals Enoteca Pinchiorri in Firenze, as do his prices. I spoke to him about you and gave a little background story, and he is most anxious to meet with you. His personal phone number is on the contact list I gave you.

"Giancarlo, Chicago is an entirely different story. It's a much more sophisticated city, as you know, having lived there. There are two Little Italies, one in the city, and then there's one in Melrose Park. Be careful there. It's a tough group, and the Sicilians control the town. I have provided you with good contacts at both locations."

I thanked Tony for his information and promised to keep him posted on developments. We concluded the evening with a little panna cotta and called it a night.

*****

November

Gina and I flew to St. Louis on a Friday morning and checked in to the Chase Hotel. It had been a long time since our last stay. I had called Angelo Oldani, the owner of Angelo's on the Hill, and we took a taxi there for an early dinner. The server was extremely attractive. I had trouble keeping from staring at her. We ordered a bottle of Brunello, and she gave me a favorable nod and winked, as if to say good choice. Gina kicked me under the table. "Giancarlo, are you all right?"

"Yes, Gina, I'm fine, just a little tired from the five-hour flight. Why do you ask?"

"Well, for a minute, you seemed a little preoccupied, and I became concerned. Did you see something you liked about the young lady who took our wine order? I think in the future, I will definitely travel with you. That way, we can rest assured your mind will stay on the reason for being on the trip."

"Gina, I may be approaching my fifty-second birthday, but I have not lost my eyesight, and besides, I stared at her to test your reaction to see if you might be a little jealous."

I got kicked again and decided to change the subject.

As Angelo approached our table, I rose to my feet to shake his hand and introduced Gina. I motioned for the waitress to pour a glass of wine for Angelo and wasted no time in starting the olive oil discussion. Initially, I could see I was getting nowhere with him.

Gina jumped in with that smile and soft-spoken approach and asked, "So, Angelo, what do you fry with?"

He quickly responded, "We deep-fry mostly."

Again, Gina went at him softly. "So if you're sautéing shrimp, chicken breast, or a veal dish of any recipe, what do you use?"

Angelo was reluctant to answer but finally said, "Lard."

I got back in and spoke with some authority about my earlier successes with restaurants in LA. Gina then spoke about the food we created at home and the improved taste. We presented him with a bottle of our oil and the challenge to test it on some of his menu. Angelo smiled and said, "Mr. Giambrone, where the hell did you find her? She is irresistible. I mean, that as a saleswoman. Leave a bottle and come back Monday night, and I'll give you my answer."

Gina looked at him and said, "Angelo, he found me about six blocks from here. I grew up on the Hill."

He was shocked. She then said, "How about you feed us tonight?"

He said, "It will be my pleasure. Nothing fried, though. I am afraid you might call the food police on me."

We all laughed.

In a matter of minutes, a small platter of fried ravioli arrived with a really good marinara sauce. It was a first for us. Angelo came over and asked if we liked the ravioli. Gina was quick to reply, "They are great, Angelo. Will you promise to serve them to us again Monday night but fried in our olive oil?"

He broke out laughing, "Giancarlo, she doesn't let up. I suggest you tie a rope around her and never let her get too far away."

Saturday night, we had reservations at Tony's. I had spoken to Vince Bommarito earlier in the week, and as soon as I mentioned Tony Bomaritto's name, the doors opened. He agreed to meet us at four, an hour before the restaurant opened.

The weather gods were kind to us. The sun was up early in the morning, and we woke up to a beautiful sunrise. Gina suggested we take an early walk to Forest Park before breakfast. There was not a soul to be seen; we had the park to ourselves. I was pensive. My mind raced back to the '20s and '30s and the trips here to visit my dear friend and mentor Elroy Phillips. He passed away in 1948 while we were in Italy, and we missed the funeral. I remembered the day I met him at the fraternity party at Princeton and his early inspiration and advice: "Giancarlo, you will meet a handful of friends while living here and in New York that will carry with you throughout your life." He and Tom Venegoni are living proof of the statement.

"Giancarlo, you're very quiet. Do you want to share your thoughts? Unless, of course, you're having fantasies about the waitress at Angelo's."

"Because you're being the curious cat that you are, I am not sharing my thoughts, smart-ass."

"Oh, come on. Be nice"

"I was thinking about my friend Elroy and the many years we came here to visit him and his family and the good times we enjoyed with them."

Gina hugged my arm and looked up at me, smiling. She understood.

There was a sign in the lobby when we returned:

> Opening tonight, two nights featuring
> Tony Bennett

"Oh, my god. Giancarlo, can we catch the show?"

"Sure, Gina. I'll call Hack the concierge and get us a table for the late show."

Our next stop was Viviano's grocers food store. On arrival, Gina said, "Wow, Giancarlo, this is the old Rau Store. It was a dry-goods and clothing store when I was a child. My mother took me here to shop for most of my clothes. It was run by a nice Jewish family."

We were both shocked at the size of the store and stood at the opening, surveying the food selections. A young man approached and asked if he could help us. I introduced Gina and myself, and he replied, "My name is Evan Severino."

"We have a meeting with Mr. Viviano."

"Please come with me. I'll take you to his office."

"Buon giorno, Signore Viviano. This is Gina, and I am Giancarlo Giambrone."

"Ah, you are Italian?"

"Well, I was born in Siracusa, Sicily, so yes, I guess you can say Italian. Tell me about this incredible store."

He laughed and said, "Signore, that's a long story. I came to this country with the clothes on my back in 1926. I started a business making bleach and later switched to making cheese, but don't ask me about that.

"Later, the Rau brothers closed this store because during the war, they couldn't get enough merchandise to sustain the overhead and also because they were getting up in the years, so I decided to rent the building in 1949 to open this store. I went to Italy and started importing Italian food products. This neighborhood is primarily first- and second-generation Italians and Sicilians who crave the food of their homeland. But today, people of all nationalities shop here from all over the city.

So, Gina, are you Italian? Gina is an Italian name."

"No, signore, I am Irish, but I was born here on the Hill about three blocks from here, and my mom used to take me to Rau Store to buy my clothes when I was a child."

"I hear that all the time. So, Giancarlo, tell me about your olive oil. We do not sell a lot of olive oil because it is too expensive. People here are very conservative. They use it sparingly on salads, never to cook with."

"Well we are trying to take care of the pricing issue. Where are you getting your oil from, and how much are you paying per liter?"

"I carry a brand from Puglia, and I order it in three-liter cans."

"We know the brand. It's a nice old firm. We have taken a different approach to marketing our oil. First, in a store your size, we rely on volume and give incentive prices and have small packaging. That way, the consumer does not have to buy a three-liter can. But first, I would like you to taste our oil."

"Let me get some bread and a dish."

Evan brought the loaf of bread and stayed briefly to watch the taste. John Viviano's eyes lit up after the first taste, and he repeated it. He invited Evan to taste, and the look on their faces told the story. "Giancarlo, you may have something here. Let me think about it."

"John, do you know Angelo Oldani? We met with him last night, and we are returning for dinner Monday night. Would you consider joining us? He is cooking with our oil, and I'd like to see your reaction."

"I'll join you but with no obligation."

Gina said, "Grazie per il tuo tempo signore. Molti piacere di cognoscenti" (Thank you for your time. It was a pleasure meeting you).

Smiling, John said, "Your Italian is as beautiful as you are, Gina. Signore Giambrone, I want both of you to know it has been a pleasure meeting you. I'll see you at Angelo's."

*****

We arrived at Tony's at four and immediately were escorted to Vince's office. The walls had autographed photos of some of the elite entertainers and politicians, including President Truman and the governor of Illinois, Adlai Stevenson. After our introduction, he asked, "So how do you know my friend Tony?"

"We belong to the same club in Palm Springs. Please tell us about the restaurant, Vince. From what we hear, it is the only five-star Italian restaurant in the country."

Smiling, Vince replied, "We are very proud of that, but maintaining that honor is a monumental task. My father opened the restaurant after the war, primarily as a spaghetti-and-meatball restaurant to serve lunch to the downtown businessmen.

"When I got involved, we decided to do the upscale version it is today by remodeling the entire restaurant and changing the menu. It was a lot of work and dedication by a lot of people. So tell me about your oil."

"First, we want to thank you for your time. Vince, my family has been in the olive oil business in Lucca for two hundred years, and we recently started importing to the US. Do you cook with olive oil?"

"As a matter of fact, we fry some dishes with it. We do not deep-fry anything in the restaurant. Because olive oil is so expensive, we use it sparingly."

"May we ask whose oil you're using and what you're paying per liter?"

"I bring it direct from Puglia in five-liter cans, and Giancarlo, no offense, I don't buy anything based on price. I want quality. The people dining in my restaurant are not price conscious.

Tony Bomaritto raved about your oil, so let's taste it, and I'll tell you in two minutes if we can do business."

The smile on his face told the story after the taste. "I love it, Giancarlo. Can you supply it to me in five-liter cans? I must be honest. I was not expecting this. We are very loyal to our purveyors."

"The answer to your question is yes. We will have special five-liter cans made to ship to you. Let me study our cost savings regarding packaging, and I'll get a price for you."

"Okay. I'll start with five cans initially because I still have inventory on the current oil we are using. If you do not have dinner plans, I'd like you to be my guests."

Gina said, "Vince, you are everything Tony told us about you, and yes, we'd love to stay for dinner."

"Follow me. I'll escort you to a table, and I'll take your order. Let me get a couple of menus."

Gina again said, "Vince, why don't you feed us?"

Candlelight lit the room, and Vince, in a matter of minutes, returned with a bottle of Livio Felluga Pinot Grigio. After pouring a glass for the three of us, he asked if we'd like to see the kitchen. We toasted each other and moved to the kitchen. It was immaculate. A man was mopping the floor, which was so clean, you could eat off it. Gina said, "Vince, I am in awe. This kitchen is so clean, a surgeon could operate in here."

"Gina, he mops washrooms from here and then returns to the kitchen and follows that routine throughout the evening. All the employees are aware of my penchant for cleanliness."

We returned to our table and were served a single cannelloni in a light marinara sauce, and Vince caught the two of us dipping our bread in it. I said, "Vince, I could make a meal of this bread and sauce."

He responded, "We make the bread and sauce fresh every day, any leftovers are given to the employees to take home. Your entrées will be here shortly."

The restaurant was soon packed. It was obvious the way people dressed spoke to the type of clientele Vince catered to. This was not the In-N-Out Burger crowd.

Our main course arrived, swordfish steaks, three-inch-thick center cut, the shape of large filet mignon, with a beurre blanc sauce that complimented the dish, along with a side of sautéed zucchini. Vince later told us he had the chef fry the zucchini with our olive oil enough so that all the cooks and he himself tasted the zucchini. It received an overwhelming vote of approval.

Vince dropped by the table while we were enjoying the swordfish, and we complimented him. We decided against dessert, and in the true Italian custom, he warmly hugged both of us as we departed. We anxiously returned to the hotel to see Tony Bennett.

After the show, as we prepared for bed, Gina said, "Giancarlo, after today's success, I must say, my concerns about the decision to bring Lucca Olive Oil to the States has changed. There is no doubt your business sense will lead to success, as has every challenge you faced over the years."

Monday's dinner at Angelo's with John Viviano was a delight. Angelo followed Gina's request, frying the ravioli in our oil, and he made eggplant parmigiana, again frying the eggplant in our oil. He also put a small dish with warmed oil on the table when our bread arrived. Both dishes were well received by John Viviano. We complimented Angelo on the meal, and when we asked for the check, he refused to take our money. Instead, he gave us a test order for our oil.

After he left, John Viviano asked about packaging, and he wrote down his information and said, "I was not considering changing brands before your arrival, but your oil and pricing have changed that. I will be sending you an order tomorrow. Thanks for including me. It has been a pleasure meeting the two of you."

Back at the hotel, packing, Gina said, "So, handsome, I noticed you hardly looked at our waitress tonight. Perhaps it was because she wasn't wearing her push-up bra." Gina could not allow the night to end without her needle.

I pretended I did not hear the question and just smiled. The push-up bra—another staple of the 1950s.

We flew back to Los Angeles the next morning, pleased with our St. Louis trip.

December

I reminded myself of Gina's wishes to avoid the olive oil business consuming our life. I asked her to make plans for the month. "Giancarlo, I spoke to Sandra the other day, and she and Tom want us to visit them in Laguna for a few days, and I agreed to drive over the middle of the month. They want to drive up to Santa Barbara and spend a couple of days. Is it all right with you?"

"Absolutely. What have you planned for the holidays?"

"We did not discuss the holidays. Let's talk about it while we're there and get the Bomarittos involved."

Santa Barbara was a delight. We stayed at the Biltmore Hotel and shared a bottle of Krug Chardonnay on our balcony and watched the sunset.

Sandra made dinner reservations at the oldest restaurant in town, Joe's Cafe. It dated back to 1928. We discussed the fact it survived prohibition, the stock market crash of '29, the depression of the '30s, and the food shortages of World War II. The food and service told the story of how that was achieved. It was so good, we elected to come back the next night.

We exchanged gifts on Christmas Eve. Tom and I agreed to cook burgers on the grill, allowing the ladies the pleasure of relaxing. Sharon and Tony had us to their house in Beverly Hills New Year's Eve, and we ushered in 1952.

CHAPTER 4

Palm Springs
January 1952

The past months had been a mix of business and relaxation. I was pleased with opening up the olive oil business in St. Louis and was eager to move ahead providing olive oil to restaurants in other locations. My friend Tony was again my go-to guy.

I met Tony for breakfast at the club, and he handed me names of restaurants and Italian specialty stores in San Francisco. Fortunately, there was a flight from Palm Springs. Gina and I flew there on a Saturday morning to enjoy the city for the weekend.

We stayed at the famed Palace Hotel. We had dinner reservations at his suggestion at Fior d'Italia, one of the oldest restaurants in the city, located in North Beach, the Italian neighborhood. It was founded in 1886. I made arrangements to meet with the owner. My approach to him was to walk softly with a laid-back pitch about Lucca Olive Oil.

I introduced Gina and myself, and he warmly greeted us and escorted us to our table. I invited him to join us after dinner. I complimented him on our meal. I explained we were in the olive oil business and asked if the chef used olive oil when frying foods. He was from Bari in Puglia and informed us he used olive oil from his hometown. He said, "Signore, we do not use olive oil for frying. It simply is too expensive. We fry with lard."

I produced a bottle of our oil for him to taste, knowing it was not going to convince him by taste alone, and after the taste, I surprised him with the price. A smile creased his face. He was shocked and said, "Can you leave the bottle so I can get with the chef and experiment with it and try a few recipes?"

I agreed and made a reservation to return Monday night.

On Sunday evening, we dined at Molinari, also on Tony's list. Founded in 1896, it was another well-respected, successful Italian restaurant. Our experience was the same, with an added benefit. We learned the family owned a major grocery store specializing in Italian food imports, and they stocked a competitor's olive oil. Our price was more competitive, and the owner was honest enough to say our oil tasted better than the oil they were using for salads. Once again, we left the bottle and made reservations for Tuesday evening to taste some of the chef's creations using our oil.

The next morning, we visited their store and were amazed at the selection of Italian foods. They had various salamis, prosciutto, and Parmigiano cheese from Parma. From the Veneto Region, they displayed Asiago cheese. Their wine selection spread across every region of Italy. In addition, their entire selection of canned tomatoes were from San Marzano. I said to Gina, "There is a better selection of Italian delicacies here than where we shop in Lucca and Siracusa. It rivals Viviano's in St. Louis."

We bought a bottle of our competitor's olive oil to bring to Lucca for our return trip. I wanted to test it to see if it truly was extra virgin, as the bottle claimed.

The next night, we returned to Fior d'Italia, and received a warm greeting from the owner. We sampled some fried eggplant, calamari, and cardoon using our oil and were delighted, as was the owner, who joined us at our table. He complimented us and asked, "How soon can you get the product to us, and what size containers do you have?"

I gave him both sizes and prices and received a nice *test* order for both.

While in the taxi back to the hotel, Gina said, "Giancarlo, when we get back to Palm Springs, I am going to sit down and design a brochure showing the different packaging and prices so you can leave it with prospective buyers. Also, you need to have business cards made. I'll work on that too."

The next night, we returned to Molinari and once again received an enthusiastic greeting. The owner insisted on providing the meal for us, which consisted of the chef's interpretation of the best uses for our oil. Price was no longer a concern due to the incentive price we had given. This was an expensive restaurant. The patrons expected the best, and price was never a concern as long as the food lived up to its reputation.

I asked the owner if we could have a small bowl of our oil for the table, which he provided. Neither Gina nor I made a statement about it but immediately dipped our bread in it. Soon, the owner was dipping his bread in it. I smiled at Gina and received a smile back from her. The owner caught the smiles and asked, "Am I missing something?"

I responded, "Signore, we have been trying to tell the restaurant owners everywhere we have dined, this is something special extra to provide for the table, especially in an upscale restaurant."

He nodded in agreement.

We were served an appetizer of baby veal meatballs fried with our oil, fried scampi with a white-wine-reduced sauce, along with a side order of angel-hair pasta served with zucchini lightly breaded and fried, again in our oil. The meal was so good, I purposely avoided discussing business while we were eating.

Once the table was cleared, we got down to business and discussed packaging for both the restaurant, three-liter cans and bottle and can sizes for the retail store. We were surprised at the size of the orders he gave us for both. These were serious, not *test* orders.

Our flight back to Palm Springs was flawless.

*****

I decided once again to focus on my promise to Gina to enjoy life. It was time to step back and enjoy the beautiful weather in the desert, play golf and tennis, and socialize with our friends.

Gina spent a good deal of time on the packaging and came up with some excellent designs for both cans and bottles. She also designed a business card for me. Her next challenge was the brochure, and her design options were excellent. She wisely told me not to include a price list in the brochure. She suggested a separate list for prices. The logic behind that was in case we decided to change prices along the way. We decided to bring the marketing materials to Lucca on our scheduled trip in April to present to our suppliers in Milan.

February

We dined at the country club and celebrated my fifty-second birthday with our friends, and Gina handed me a large gift-wrapped box. After dinner and birthday cake, the group sang "Happy Birthday." I opened the box, only to find inside another smaller box, and inside was another smaller box, which I opened, and found a Rolex gold watch. That prompted a hug and a kiss, as she whispered in my ear, "You get the rest of your presents when we get home later."

I whispered back, "Can you give me a hint?"

"No, wild man. Calm down."

CHAPTER 5

Lucca
April

The past few months were filled with creative ideas for packaging, marketing, and distributing our oil. We were excited and optimistic about selling it in Italy.

We flew to Rome and connected with a flight to Firenze, and Salvatore drove us to Lucca. It was a joyous greeting with Anna, who took a loaf of fresh bread from the oven as we entered the kitchen. On the table was a small dish of olive oil, and Anna sliced the bread, brushed a few slices with the oil, lightly sprinkled salt and pepper on them, and popped them back in the oven for a couple of minutes. Then she put the bread on the table and stood to watch us devour it.

She said, "I have been experimenting with different recipes frying and cooking with olive oil and testing the dishes on some of the employees for lunch, and I believe you will enjoy them. I still have that age-old concern in my mind about the expense. I have been cooking with lard my entire life, as did my mother and my grandmother before me. It is difficult to change old methods, but I must admit, there is a difference. Proof of that was watching the employees enjoying what I cooked the past few months."

We were making progress.

Despite the ambiance of Lucca, my mind was consumed by the advancement the Chinese and North Korean forces were making in the war. The United Nations had organized the armies of sixteen nations to fight the North Koreans and the Chinese. The brunt of expense was borne by the US.

Casualties among the Americans and Allied forces were mounting. I felt our government was asleep. Nothing was being done to reach a settlement to the conflict. The fact remains we essentially were at war with China.

Gina, always alert when my mind was occupied, came and rescued me. "Can I get your attention for a minute, sir? When are we going to Milan to put my packaging ideas to bed?"

"Yes, master, let's make a few calls and set up appointments immediately. It will require two trips, one to initiate the interpretation of your designs and a return to finalize them."

On Monday the following week, we drove to Milan and checked in to the famed Hotel Gallia. We dined at our favorite restaurant, Antico Trattoria della Pesa, and received a warm reception. The owner arrived at our table almost at the time we were seated. He brought a bottle of Brunello with his compliments. While he was pouring the wine, our waiter brought the traditional baby veal meatballs. I toasted the owner and said, "Allora Signore, I have a question. Do you fry the *polpette* in olive oil?"

Gina kicked me under the table. He looked at me as if to say, "Are you crazy?" His reply said it all. "Signore, this restaurant has been in my family since 1888. We have always fried those meatballs in lard. You and our guests have been eating them forever, and we have never heard a complaint. It is too expensive to fry with olive oil, so we use it only in our salad dressing."

I got another kick from Gina and elected to drop the subject. She later said, "Giancarlo, do you ever stop?"

The next day, we met with our packaging designers and submitted Gina's work and exchanged ideas for the bottles and cans and walked away feeling good about their reaction.

The next stop was the printer. Here, too, her designs for the brochure and business card were well received. We were told to go to lunch and return at five, and they would have the first proofs for us.

We had lunch at the hotel, and I made a call to our distributor and set up an appointment for the next day. It was one of those warm sunny spring days, and we decided to take a walk. The sun was bright, not a cloud to be seen.

As was always the case, Milan seemed like it was in a hurry to succeed in leading Italy's recovery from the rampages of World War II. It was contagious. One could sense it in the restaurants the way businesspeople were engaged in conversation. Food was not the reason they were there.

We returned at five to view the early printed samples of Gina's designs for the brochure and were pleased. We gave them the green light to proceed with the samples and asked them to send them to us for final approval. We decided to dine at the hotel that evening.

The next day, we returned to the packaging office and viewed the initial bottle and can samples and were pleased and gave them an order. We met with our distributor, and once again received a cool reception. Gina made the presentation using the proofs for the brochure and the bottle and can samples. She made a great presentation and received a warm reception.

I followed with our lower incentive pricing, and that really warmed the meeting. The owner said, "Well, Giancarlo, this changes things. It is evident you are serious about marketing your oil. Please, as soon as the packaging and brochure are ready, send us samples for our sales team, and we will aggressively begin to sell your oil. We are on board."

We returned to Lucca satisfied. We experienced a major achievement and turned the page for the second stage of the business.

Once again, I decided to relax and pay tribute to Gina for her contribution for the brochure and her designs for the cans and bottles. "Giancarlo, I would like to take a trip to Siena. We have never visited it. Everything I have read about the city has intrigued me, especially the history. There is an annual horse race called Palio, and it attracts crowds from all over Italy."

"Gina, check on when they have the race, and let's plan on being there."

We went to see the movie, *Singin' in the Rain* with Gene Kelly and Debbie Reynolds. It won an academy award earlier in the year. We were amazed at the production and talent. It truly deserved the Academy Award.

I began reading *The Silver Chalice* by Tom Chastain, which is about the supposed chalice Jesus used at the Last Supper. It occupied my time and took my mind off the olive oil business and the war.

Gina brought home a few new records, including Fats Domino's "Goin' Home" and Kay Starr's "Wheel of Fortune." Also in the mix was Lloyd Price's "Lawdy Miss Clawdy" and his rendition of "Night Train." Things were picking up in the music world. The most important movement was with black singers and musicians.

*****

Salvatore Vitale came to see me with a suggestion. He was timid and somewhat intimidated but managed to voice what was on his mind. "Signore, we can improve the quality of the oil and increase the volume by getting more from each press with the new presses that are available. They are expensive, but if you want a better product I truly believe it is necessary.

Our current presses date back to the 1930s, and they are beginning to show wear, and we spend a lot of time repairing them, and parts are getting hard to find, which consumes more of my time searching for them."

I thanked him for his time and placed a call to Milan to the supplier producing the new presses. They promised a salesman would call us in the near future.

May

As promised, the press salesman came calling and showed us the brochure of the latest presses. After hearing the presentation by the salesman, we were convinced we could produce a higher-quality extra virgin oil and increase the yield. Salvatore and I placed an order for them. Gina attended the meeting and later questioned the expense. "Gina, if we are going to do this, we must understand there will be expenses. You have to spend money to make money. I am not concerned about the costs."

"But, Giancarlo, don't you think you should increase the business first before spending the money for new presses?"

"The business will come, Gina, especially if we increase the quality of the oil."

I decided it was time to visit our distributor in Bologna. Gina agreed to join me and suggested while we were in that part of Italy we should visit the great city of Parma. Both cities were renowned for the food served in the restaurants.

We drove to Bologna and checked in to the Grand Hotel Majestic già Baglioni for two days. We had dinner that night at Osteria del Sole. Founded in 1465, it was the oldest restaurant in the city. Gina was shocked when I told her its age.

After dinner, I asked the manager to come to our table and handed him a brochure and told him about our oil. He politely explained that purchasing food for the restaurant was not his position but agreed to give the brochure to the person who did the purchasing

The next morning, we met with Angelo Salerno, the owner of the distributor we had used for years. He was the second generation of the firm, which dated back to the early days of the century. Gina made the presentation of the brochure and the new packaging, and I followed up with lower prices. I presented a bottle of oil, sample bottles, and a three-liter can. "Well, Gina and Giancarlo, I must say I am pleasantly surprised. I was not expecting this.

"No one from your firm has been here in years, nor have we had the tools to sell your oil. Price has always been a problem to do any serious business. We never could make enough money to sustain a business. For that reason, we sell various cheeses, canned tomatoes, and prosciutto and salami from Parma. I can't promise anything major for the future, but we will get behind the product with renewed enthusiasm. We appreciate your taking the time to visit."

Gina and I took the rest of the day to visit my alma mater at the University of Bologna. She was overwhelmed by the fact it was the oldest university in the world, founded in 1088.

We drove to Parma the next morning and checked in to the hotel Palazzo Dalla Rosa Prati. "Giancarlo, how did you hear about this hotel?"

"Why do you ask?"

"Because it is not your style. It is pretty old and worn, don't you think?"

"Well, Ms. Giambrone, we're only here for tonight. Let's go for a walk. It's a beautiful day, and we should take advantage of the nice weather and see some of the city. We do not have a dinner reservation. Let's see if we can find a nice, expensive restaurant to spend some of the money we are saving by staying in this cheap hotel."

"Are you trying to make me look bad because I complained about the hotel, Mr. Giambrone? You just agreed to spend thousands of dollars on new presses for the olive oil business. Perhaps you booked this inexpensive hotel to save money."

"I refuse to challenge that statement. You are digging yourself a deep hole. It will require a big shovel to dig your way out."

"Mr. Giambrone, good plan not to challenge. There is no couch in the room for you to sleep in, and the tub in the bathroom is tiny. Let's go for that walk."

All I could do was smile.

We walked the beautiful tree-lined streets of the famous city. I gave Gina a brief history, having studied it while a student at U of Bologna. It dated back to the early Romans, who founded it in AD 183.

Our walk carried us to an old piazza, Piazza Garibaldi, named after the famed Italian general who helped organize the unification of Italy in 1861. We stumbled on a restaurant that looked interesting called Antica Osteria della Ghiaia. It was closed, but we liked the menu on the door and decided to return for dinner. That night we were grateful, we found it. The food lived up to everything we had heard about the city's gastronomic reputation.

The next morning, while Gina was packing, I went to see the concierge and had him call our distributor in Verona, Pietro Balsorati. He agreed to meet us that afternoon. I paid the bill, went back to the room, and told Gina our change of plans.

The short drive through the countryside was delightful, complemented by beautiful weather. The concierge suggested we stay at Due Torri hotel and was kind enough to call and reserve a room for us. When we arrived, I called Pietro, and he joined us for lunch. I continued my practice, avowing not to discuss business while dining. We spent the entire lunch hour learning about his family background and that of the company.

Once the table was cleared, I directed the conversation to Gina, who did an excellent job presenting the brochure and photos of the new packaging. "Thank you, Signora. I like the new brochure and packaging. I presume you will be sending samples of both for us to use in selling the oil. But, Signore Giambrone, you have to understand what we are up against when it comes to price. First of all, the oil coming from Puglia is less expensive than your oil."

I allowed him to speak, and when he was finished, I went at him with our new price lists. He was aghast. His face lit up with a smile ear to ear. Then I asked the waiter to bring a small bowl to the table and some fresh bread and asked him to dip the bread and taste the oil. Mission accomplished. He gave us a test order on the spot and invited us to be his guest for dinner that evening at Ristorante Ponte Pietra.

Back at the hotel, Gina looked at me and said, "Well, Mr. Giambrone, if I may say so myself, I think we make a great team. What do you think?"

"Yes, and you might add you're very modest about it too."

"Now who is digging the hole, junior?"

We had agreed to meet Pietro at seven and arrived a few minutes early. The restaurant was small. I was following Gina, who was walking behind the waiter heading to our table. Shortly before we arrived at the table, I heard a loud, "Giancarlo."

I could not believe my eyes. It was my college sweetheart Lidia Provenzano. It had been thirty-two years since I last saw her. She jumped out of her chair and threw both arms around me, kissed me on both sides of my face, and tearfully hugged me for a good five minutes.

My memory of our last time together flashed back to the day I departed for New York from Rome in 1919. It was one of the most emotional moments of my life. We parted in tears. I believe things would have been different if I had stayed in Italy, perhaps marrying

Lidia. She looked great. I quickly calculated she was fifty-one years old and compared her looks to Gina, who was ten years younger. Lidia looked good, but there was no doubt I made the right choice with Gina.

Gina turned around and I introduced her to Lidia. "Gina and Giancarlo, this is my friend Stefano Brusati. Please join us."

I explained we were meeting a friend. Pietro walked in and saw us and came over. I made the introduction and excused ourselves, and we went to our respective tables. Gina winked and whispered, "We will be discussing this when we get back to the hotel."

All I could do was smile. I knew I would have some explaining to do when we returned to the hotel. I was prepared, having told Gina about her in the past.

Our dinner was exceptional, and we returned to the hotel, content with our decision to come to Verona. As soon as we walked in the room, Gina's sharp wit and needle surfaced, and she commented about the reception I received from Lidia. "Well, I'll say one thing about you, Mr. Giambrone. When you love them, they stay loved and never forget you!"

I refused to reply.

"Come on, junior. Let's have it." Laughing, she said, "I assume you are not answering me because you have seen the size of the tub, and you choose to sleep beside me tonight, but don't be expecting anything but sleep."

"Your memory, Ms. Cat, deceives you. Is it possible age is causing convenient memory loss? I distinctly remember telling you early on that Lidia was my first serious girlfriend. We met at U of Bologna when I was a sophomore. She was a freshman. That's it."

"Oh, no, Romeo. Let's hear about the romance. Were you in love? Did you travel with her? How did it end? And don't leave out the details about hotel accommodations!"

"What are you doing? Is this some book you are writing?"

"Yes, I have been thinking about doing just that. I even have the title: *GG's Conquests: The Many Loves of One of the World's Great Lovers.*"

"You'll have to find another cowriter, lady. As of this moment, I resign. My lips are sealed. A gentleman never discloses his love life."

"Ah, gee, just as it was starting to get good."

*****

Our drive through the Veneto countryside was like a documentary on the beauty of the region. The road was mostly along Lake Garda, and we stopped in Sirmione for lunch and dined alfresco with a beautiful view of the lake. It was a day to remember, with little conversation during the meal. I sat and stared at Gina as she studied the conto for the meal, grateful for the day I met her.

We spent the night again in Milan and departed early the next morning for Lucca.

Lucca
June

We departed for the drive to Siena and arrived in time for lunch. The plan was to spend the day and travel to San Gimignano to spend the night. We saw people eating alfresco and took a table along the rail overlooking the beautiful piazza directly opposite the cathedral.

A waiter approached us and handed us a simple lunch menu. I allowed Gina the pleasure of ordering. The waiter had already qualified us as American tourists, especially because Gina didn't look Italian. She shocked him with her Italian when she ordered. Speaking so fast, he was having trouble writing her requests. He smiled and looked at Gina and, in English, said, "Madam, your Italian is perfect. I will make a special effort to ensure your lunch is as good as your Italian."

Gina smiled and said, "Grazie, signore."

The food lived up to his promise.

We later walked the city and marveled at the cleanliness. We learned the piazza where we had lunch was called Piazza del Campo, and it is where they have the annual Palio horse race. The race dates back to 1482 and is held semiannually. The next one, scheduled for July, conflicted with our trip to Siracusa.

We went into the duomo, and Gina lit a candle honoring Giuseppe. We decided to head to San Gimignano.

We checked in to the Hotel Collegiata and learned from the concierge that it had been a fifteenth-century monastery. We asked her to make dinner reservations for us at a restaurant I had read about called Le Vecchie Mura. Gina unpacked for us, and we drove to the city center.

Most of the walls date back to the 16th century, long before the unification of Italy. They were used to defend the town during the inner-city wars.

We walked the town and loved the towers. Gina elected to climb the stairs to the top along with another tourist.

We completed our tour of the historical city and walked to the restaurant for dinner. We sat at a table overlooking the entire valley. It was a memorable photo, which included the happy people surrounding us. The food and service lived up to the article I had read.

As we departed, Gina said, "I must compliment you, Giancarlo. Not once at any of the restaurants did you mention Lucca Olive Oil. Did you forget we are in the business?"

The drive through the Tuscan hills was breathtaking. We were both pensive with limited conversation. Only toward the end did Gina ask, "Giancarlo, why so quiet?"

"I was going to ask you the same question. For me, it was the scenery and how fortunate we are to have the best of both worlds, living here six months of the year and six months in Palm Springs."

"I was on that same path, thinking about the two days, and how lucky I was to meet you and the lifestyle you have created for me."

"Lifestyle for us, Gina. I get to enjoy it too."

*****

July

Our trip to Siracusa was approaching, and as had become tradition, I walked out on the patio for one last look at the forest of olive trees. Salvatore loaded the car for the trip to Firenze for our flight to Catania. I spent most of the drive reminiscing about the previous three months.

"So, Giancarlo, are you excited to get to Siracusa?"

"I am, Gina. What do you have planned to entertain me? I'm sure that overactive brain of yours is already in overdrive to keep my mind off the war and the olive oil business."

"Well, as a matter of fact, once we are settled, I'd like you to take me to Taormina. How does that sound?"

"I think it's a great idea. Let's do it. My plan for us is to relax, see a few good movies, and read. As promised, I have no desire to try to sell our oil in Sicily. Let's enjoy our three months. I can't wait to get there."

Vincenzo drove us to Siracusa and told us Alena was preparing a surprise for lunch. She greeted Gina with a hug and, for the first time ever, did the same to me. The table on the balcony was already set, with an opened bottle of white wine. Warm bread and a dish of olive oil was present. Soon, Alena arrived with eggplant fried with olive oil, baby veal meatballs served with a marinara sauce also fried with olive oil, and assorted vegetables fried the same way.

Gina thanked her, and we proceeded to devour the feast. I was eating with both hands, and Gina grabbed them and said, "Giancarlo, slow down. You're eating like you're scheduled to face the electric chair in the morning and this is your last meal."

I laughed and did as she asked. It was a meal to remember, as was the day. The bright sunshine made it complete.

The next morning, we went into town for coffee and walked to the movie theater. *High Noon* with Gary Cooper and Grace Kelly was playing, and we decided to see it that night. But first, we would have an early dinner. "Giancarlo, you're being very quiet. What's going on in that inquisitive mind of yours?"

"I'm thinking we can't make any serious money with the small orders we are getting from the restaurants and the specialty grocery stores. I want to focus on the current distributors in Italy and establish additional ones. That's my goal in the States when we get back.

In addition, once we have more distribution here in Italy and in the US, we need to do some advertising, which will separate us from other olive oil producers."

"I agree, Giancarlo. When we get back to Palm Springs, I'll work on networking with people we already are selling to see if they have local food distributors they can recommend."

*****

The next day, we drove to Taormina in a rainstorm, but as we neared the city center, the rain ceased. We checked in to the Grand Hotel San Pietro and asked the concierge to make reservations for us at Ristorante Cinque Archi that night and, for the next two nights, at Ristorante al Paladino and Granduca Ristorante.

Taormina is a picturesque city located on the eastern coast of Sicily, perched on a hill overlooking the Ionian Sea. Known for its stunning views, it boasts a blend of ancient ruins, medieval architecture, and vibrant cultural life. Its key attractions include the ancient Greek Theatre, which offers panoramic views of Mount Etna and the sea, and the charming Corso Umberto—a bustling street filled with shops, cafes, and historical buildings. Taormina's beautiful beaches, such as Isola Bella, and its lush gardens add to its appeal as a popular tourist destination.

"Giancarlo, how did you know about this incredible hotel and those restaurants?"

"My parents brought me here when I graduated from secondary school, and we stayed at this hotel and had dinner at those restaurants."

"And one more question, my world traveler: during those wild bachelor years, did you bring any of your conquests here and live in sin in this hotel?"

"I refuse to answer on the grounds of risking your judgment, Ms. Curiosity Cat."

We unpacked and walked to the famous theater built by the Greeks over seven hundred years before Christ was born. We had a brochure from the hotel that gave a brief history of the city. It too, dated back to the same period. I tried to imagine what life was like when they built the theater.

We took a leisurely walk around town, blessed by incredible warm weather. We found a small trattoria for lunch and had a simple plate of pasta with a lobster sauce and a carafe of wine. We enjoyed the rest of the afternoon at the hotel pool. My mind drifted back to 1918, when I was last here with my parents. I asked myself, *Where did those thirty four years go?*

The next day, the rain gods kept us indoors at the hotel but let up in time for our walk to dinner. As is always the case in Sicily, our dinner was exceptional.

Early the next morning, we departed for our return to Siracusa.

October

Back in Siracusa, I sent a cable to our distributor Marco Pelligrino in Rome, who agreed to meet us prior to the return flight to New York. After introductions, Gina presented the brochure, and I put a bottle of oil on the table for him to taste. I could tell he liked the presentation, but he was silent.

Both of us were disappointed at his lack of enthusiasm. I finally said, "Signore, we have not had any business from you in years. What do we have to do to renew the relationship?"

"Signore Giambrone, this is the first time anyone from your firm has taken the time to visit us since before the war. That happened to be Giuseppe Fragale. He was a nice man.

"We have been buying oil from a company in Puglia, and the price is better than what we used to pay for your oil. However, I must admit the oil I just tasted is better. It looks like a better press. I also am impressed with both your packaging and new prices. We have enough inventory from our current supplier for now, but I will give you an order for three cases of the quarter-liter bottles. We need samples for our sales people to leave with our clients and see how they react. Can you please include in the shipment brochures and the price list. Send enough copies for our fifteen salesmen."

"Grazie, Signore Pelligrino. Please allow me to apologize for the past. Unfortunately, Giuseppe passed away recently. We promise you better service in the future. Here is my card. It has my personal phone number. Feel free to call me in the future. Thank you for your time and the order. We appreciate both. We will be here once a year, and if you are ever in Tuscany from April through June, please come visit us. We spend those three months in Lucca there every year."

Our flight to New York the next day was a delight, especially after the successful meeting with Signore Pelligrino. We were happy to be going home to Palm Springs.

*****

Palm Springs
November

The country was embroiled in the election. Dwight Eisenhower, a popular general of World War II, was running against the governor of Illinois, Adlai Stevenson, an articulate, well-educated politician. Eisenhower pledged to end the war in Korea. He blamed it on the Democrats, stating they were doing nothing to end it.

Stevenson campaigned on his experience as governor running the government of the state of Illinois. In addition, he was the former ambassador to the United Nations, stressing his exposure and experience in world events. He also had spent many years working for the federal government in DC. His criticism of Eisenhower was that his only claim to fame was in the military.

Eisenhower won the election and became the thirty-fourth president of the US. He immediately requested US diplomats to initiate negotiations to end the war in Korea. He also pledged to the American people he would avoid any future wars.

We celebrated Thanksgiving at the club with the Venegonis and the Bomarittos. The conversation centered on both Korea and the country's increased involvement in Vietnam. Sandra said, "Okay, gentlemen, that's enough politics and wars. In case you have not noticed, there are three beautiful ladies sitting here."

The weather in the desert in December was incredibly warm. We played a lot of golf and tennis. The holidays crept up on us, and the six of us celebrated New Year's Eve at Melvin's, a fine restaurant in town. We welcomed 1953 with hugs and kisses.

CHAPTER 6

Palm Springs
January 1953

I was reading the paper and savoring my morning coffee when the phone rang. "Good morning, Giancarlo. It's Tony. Do you have a few minutes?"

"Sure, Tony. What's up?"

"I would like you to drive to LA and meet Sam Marzullo. He owns Marzullo Food and Cheese. He does business with most of the food purveyors in California. I got his name from one of my restaurant purveyors. I have spoken to him about your olive oil, and he is interested in talking to you, but he wants exclusive distribution rights for the entire state, or he refuses to meet."

"Tony, I will be happy to meet with him. However, he must show that he is qualified to build the business to earn an exclusive. My next two weeks are open. Please set something up for lunch. I want him to taste the oil."

"Thanks, Tony. You know how much I appreciate this. See you on the golf course Saturday."

Later that afternoon, I discussed the call with Gina, and she agreed it was the correct direction. "Giancarlo, if it works out, the real benefit is we will not have to carry inventory to supply the entire state. It eliminates a staff of office and warehouse employees. The last thing we want to do is move to LA to run the business"

"Gina, I couldn't agree more. Let's cook some pasta for dinner. Why don't you start the sauce. I'll open a bottle of wine and put some music on."

"Okay. Put on the new record 'I Apologize' by Billy Eckstine. There's also one by Tony Bennett, 'Rags to Riches.' Do you want long pasta or penne?"

"Surprise me."

The phone rang. It was Tony. "Giancarlo, we are on with Sam Marzullo this Friday for lunch. He has a place in the desert and will meet us at our club at noon."

"Wow, that was fast, Tony. I presume you will be presenting me with a bill for this if we strike a deal."

"You're kidding, of course. I know you'd do anything for me, Giancarlo. All I ask is to sit at your table and dine on one of Gina's great meals. Enjoy your evening. See you Friday"

Gina raised her glass of wine and said, "Here's to your meeting Friday, Giancarlo. I know you'll dazzle him with your brilliance. I can assure you he doesn't get up early enough in the morning to outshine you."

"Wow, Gina, where did that come from?"

"Eat your pasta, Junior, or I will not serve the surprise dessert sitting in the refrigerator."

"Speaking of pasta, do you ever think about the fact that we dine in the finest restaurants in LA and Italy, and nothing is any better than a simple plate of pasta with a little marinara sauce?"

"So my pasta is simple now?"

"Tell me about the surprise in the refrigerator."

"No, you have to first dig yourself out of the hole you just dug."

"Gina, I paid you a compliment. Your pasta is as good as any meal we share in the best restaurants."

"Good, that was some fast shoveling. You're back on track for the cannoli."

*****

On Friday, I was the first to arrive at the club for the meeting with Tony and Sam. I had the waiter bring a small plate and some warmed bread to dip into our olive oil. I also asked him to open a bottle of wine. Tony arrived with Sam and made the introduction.

The waiter saw their arrival and quickly came over and poured the wine. I dipped some bread in the olive oil. We toasted each other, and I invited Tony and Sam to dip their bread. Sam tasted the bread, smiled, and said, "Giancarlo, this is a good start. I like the oil and the wine. Tell me about your olive oil business."

"Sam, I have a rule. I hope you don't mind. I enjoy talking about business after the meal. Let's order some lunch and get to know each other first, and then we'll discuss the oil."

Laughing, Sam said, "Tony, he's smooth. He wants to wine and dine me, get me in a content mood, and swoop in for the kill."

I said, "You *busted* me, Sam. You got up early this morning and had me figured out before we met."

After lunch, Sam answered my questions about his business experience gained over his twenty years in the food business. He proudly spoke about his staff and the history of his firm. I made the presentation using the brochure and packaging and showed a few bottles and can samples. Next, I surprised him with the special incentive pricing I put together for distributors to cover overhead and profit.

"Well, Giancarlo, I must be honest. I am pleasantly pleased. One last question: do I get exclusive rights for the state of California?"

"Yes, Sam. I brought a simple one-page five-year agreement to review with your attorney. It consists of a five-year option based on an increase each year in volume."

"Giancarlo, I can read. Let me see it. I don't need to have my attorney read it."

In a matter of minutes, Sam asked the waiter for a pen, and we signed the agreement. We concluded the lunch and toasted each other. Sam left, and I gave Tony a hug, thanked him, and invited him and Sharon for dinner Saturday night.

Later, the Venegoni's arrived to spend the weekend with us, and I shared the news about the deal with Sam Marzullo. After dinner Tony, Tom, and I moved to our den, and we laid out a plan for finding distributors across the country. We decided there should be one for the Midwest, either Chicago or St. Louis, and one for New York. For the Northeast, we selected Boston. For the Southeast, we chose

JOE REINA

Atlanta, with Dallas for the southwest. Thus, those became my travel plans for the next few months before leaving for Lucca at the end of March.

At bedtime, Gina asked about my time with Tom, and I told her about my plan. She did not comment. The silence continued when we got in bed. I said, "Okay, sweetheart, what's the problem?"

"There's no problem. Perhaps as you travel throughout the country for the next three months, you can rent apartments in each of those cities. That way, when we get back from Italy next November, you can go visit the clients and spend some quality time with them. I'm sure I can find something to do to occupy my time."

"Come on, Gina. We both agreed the best way to build the business was through distributors."

"I know, Mr. Supersalesman, but does it have to be overnight? The business has been there for two hundred years, and it isn't like you need the money."

"Let's go to sleep. This is not the time to solve this problem." I knew enough not to continue the discussion and decided to sleep, but it was a sleepless night.

Gina was quiet the next morning, and I decided to discuss the situation before the Venegonis arose. "Gina, I thought about our discussion in my sleepless night, and I agree. You are right. We still have a life. So what do you think of my revised plan? I will make a trip to Chicago. I'd like you to join me. We have not been there for five years. As for the rest of the plan, we'll let it sit and take it one day at a time when we return in the fall from Italy."

"Well, that sounds good. Now you'll have the pleasure of hearing my jovial voice instead of the silent treatment I had planned for you for the next three months."

"Get over here and hug me, you devil."

*****

Sandra and Tom came in as we were embracing, and Sandra said, "Oops, are we interrupting something here? Should we return to our room?"

52

Gina replied, "No, Sandra. Giancarlo just dodged a major explosion and begged forgiveness after being down on his knees, and as always, I forgave him with a hug."

The weekend was highlighted by a great dinner Gina prepared Saturday night. Sharon and Tony joined us.

Monday I was back in the olive oil mood, and Gina was on my case. "Giancarlo, I know this trip to Chicago is on your mind, so let's plan on it today. I'll make plane and hotel reservations for us. You start making appointments with the people on Tony's list. Should I set up restaurant meeting places too?"

"Please, Gina. That way, we can justify the expense for your joining me."

She chased me all the way down the hall to the bedroom. I let her catch me, grabbed her, and kissed her. When it ended, she said, "Don't get any ideas, wild man. Get on the phone and start making appointments."

I had a tough time cold-calling those on Tony's list. Some refused to see me; others agreed with no promise to buy anything. This was not like the reception I received in St. Louis. I discussed it with Gina, and she reminded me, "Chicago is a tough, competitive market, Giancarlo. Maybe you should be searching for a distributor as opposed to spending time with restaurants and Italian special-ty-food stores."

"I agree, Gina. My hope was to find food purveyors through them and possibly the top distributors. The best chance of getting the right distributor is by recommendations from the restaurants and purveyors. We have to start somewhere."

I made enough appointments to justify the trip, and Gina did her part, and we departed for the Windy City. We checked in to the Ritz-Carlton and headed to Gene and Georgetti's for dinner. Tony the maître d' remembered us warmly and seated us. He came to our table after we ordered, and I wasted no time asking if they fried with olive oil. He laughed and said, "Mr. Giambrone, you must be kidding. We deep-fry just about everything in lard. Why do you ask?"

After explaining our business, I cut to the chase and asked who the restaurant's top purveyor was. He wrote down the firm and the owner's name and phone number.

Our meeting the next morning was with the owner of the top Italian food-specialty store on Taylor Street. We received a nice reception and were impressed with the food selections and the cheeses and wine. The place was packed. Gina presented the brochure and packaging, and I put oil on a small dish for the taste. Next, I presented the price list.

"Mr. Giambrone, this is superior olive oil to what we carry, and your prices are competitive, but if you want to break into the Chicago market, you need a good distributor. How long will you be in town?"

"We will be here until we find the right distributor."

"Let me contact mine. He is a good guy. Let me see if I can set up a meeting. His name is Sal Vinceguerra. Where are you staying?"

"We are at the Ritz. Thank you, Michael."

Our next appointment was Tufano's restaurant for lunch. After lunch, the owner sat with us, and Gina did her thing with the brochure and packaging, and he tasted the oil. I gave him the price list to review. "The oil is great. The truth of the matter is we do not use olive oil to cook with. We fry with lard or deep-fry. Your prices are better, and the oil is better than what we are currently buying. Do you have a distributor in Chicago?"

"We do not, Signore Tufano. Can you recommend one?"

"Yes. His name is Vinceguerra. Let me find his card for his phone number. Everyone loves Sal."

For dinner, we went to Pompei on Taylor Street. The owner had our favorite old table ready for us. It was coming home. I wasted no time and asked the usual question about what was used for frying. When I suggested using olive oil, we received the same answer we had been hearing—it was too expensive. Gina said, "Giancarlo, why are you wasting time trying to convince small restaurants to fry with oil?"

"Gina, they are the grass roots. It has to start with them, next are the purveyors, and they have to convince the distributors to carry the inventory. Another factor is the patrons in the restaurants. Once they get a taste of food fried with olive oil, they will go to the specialty stores and begin frying with it. That's the domino effect for establishing demand."

"Handsome, did anyone ever tell you you're a genius?"

"Yes, my lovely bride, I hear it all the time."

"Well, it's nice to know you're modest about it."

*****

The next morning, there was a message waiting for us at the front desk from Michael at the food store. It read,

> Call Sal Vinceguerra, I told him about your
> olive oil, he is interested and wishes to meet with
> you and Gina.

I placed the call to Sal and made arrangements to meet for lunch that day at Tufano's. Gina and I purposely arrived early, and I arranged to get the check for lunch and asked Mr. Tufano to join us during the meal. At my request, he brought a small dish for the oil and a basket of crusty warmed Italian bread.

Sal arrived, and after introductions, we ordered lunch. I peppered Sal about his family origin and learned they were from Tuscany. he knew Lucca and had been there. Without saying a word, Gina and I began dipping our bread in the oil. Soon, he was doing it too. Sal started smiling, "So, you two, I presume you assumed I was born yesterday. You put your olive oil on the table, enticing me to taste before we even discussed business. Well, it worked. The oil is great. Tell me about it."

"Sal, are you in a hurry?"

"No, why?"

"We asked Signore Tufano to fry a few appetizers with our oil, and we'd like your opinion before we have lunch."

Before long, a waiter brought baby veal meatballs, eggplant sliced thinly, and sautéed spinach to the table. Signore Tufano brought a bottle of wine, poured our glasses, and joined us. The food was superb. The look on Sal's face said it all. There was no doubt he was impressed.

It was Gina's turn to push the button. She was motivated with Sal's reception of the food. Her presentation even excited me.

Signore Tufano left so we could talk privately, and I produced our distributor prices, and Sal acknowledged they were acceptable. "So, Giancarlo, I'm sure you realize I have to have exclusive distribution rights. What's my territory? I do business in Illinois, Indiana, Wisconsin, Iowa, and Michigan."

"Sal, those states are agreeable to me. I brought the contract with me for you to review. It's a simple five-year deal with a five-year option based on a graduated increase in volume. I'll add the States to it. Please review it with your attorney, and perhaps we can meet before we leave Chicago to sign it."

Smiling, Sal said, "Giancarlo, I am surprised. You and Gina have sold me. Don't you want to move in for the kill? I don't need to meet with my lawyer. I've seen enough. I love your oil and the two of you. I will meet you for breakfast in the morning and bring an opening order based on what the contract requires. I say we need to toast our deal."

The next morning, we concluded the deal with a satisfactory purchase order and had breakfast. "Sal it has been a pleasure, and if ever in Tuscany, please let us know. We'd love to have you visit us and dine at our villa. We also have extra bedrooms, and you're welcome to stay with us." We shook hands, and he departed.

Later that morning, we checked out of the hotel, but before we left, I called Michael at the food-specialty store and Signore Tufano and thanked them for their help and passed on the news that Sal was our distributor.

*****

February

Gina was quiet at breakfast. After clearing the table, she said, "I need some time alone. I am going for a walk."

I decided to let it sit until she returned. My curiosity got the best of me. I racked my brain to recall anything I might have said or done to bring this on.

It was nearing time for lunch, and I decided to prepare a couple of sliced turkey sandwiches as she walked in the door. Once again, silence prevailed while we ate. I finally said, "Gina, I don't have a clue as to what I have done to deserve this silence. Please tell me what's bothering you."

"Giancarlo, you have not done anything."

Before I could say anything, she began crying. "At my recent annual physical, Dr. Correnti discovered a small lump in my right breast. I had not noticed it because it is so small. He inserted a needle in order to do a biopsy and said not to be too concerned.

When we returned from our trip, there was a note from him, stating he tried to call while we were away, and asked me to call him immediately. I reached him late yesterday, and he told me the bad news. I have breast cancer, Giancarlo!"

Tears were flowing like a faucet as she leaped into my arms. I no longer controlled my emotions and began crying. We were in a bear hug. I did not know what to say. We just hugged for a while.

We finally separated, and she calmly related the next procedure. "Dr. Correnti said I will be having what is called a lumpectomy to remove the cancer. He also said he is sure we caught it early. He wants me to see a plastic surgeon for removal of the lump."

"Oh my god, Gina, I don't know what to say."

"Say a prayer, Giancarlo. We just have to hope it is confined and has not spread to my lymph glands."

"When are you planning to have the surgery?"

"I have an appointment with the surgeon tomorrow. Will you go with me? I'm scared, Giancarlo."

"Gina, I will be next to you until you have made a complete recovery. I will not leave your side."

"It's the unknown right now that is driving me insane, but I have great confidence in Dr. Correnti. I hope the surgeon is as good as Correnti says he is."

The following week, we met with Dr. Terry Sullivan, the surgeon. He was very pleasant and took his time explaining the procedure. He took a pencil and drew a half-moon circle line on a piece of paper and said the line represented the size of the incision. "Gina, I have studied the biopsy. You have nothing to worry about. We will send tissue from the lump to our pathology department while you are on the operating table to be sure we got it all. Once we have been assured, you will move to a special room so we can monitor you the rest of the day. As long as there are no complications, you will be going home in three or four days. We may elect to do some minor radiation after we study the pathology report. Do you have any questions?"

"Doctor, please don't think I am vain, but how bad will the scar be?"

Smiling, Dr. Sullivan said, "Not even your husband will be able to detect it. Gina, if it's agreeable, I would like to schedule the operation for next Tuesday."

"Doctor, I would have you do it this afternoon. I want to get it over with."

"Stay calm, Gina. I have a few patients waiting for the same procedure. I'll see you next week. I want you to rest."

I tried to keep Gina in a positive frame of mind. We went to see the movie *Roman Holiday* with Audrey Hepburn and Gregory Peck. I bought the book *Love Is Eternal* by Irving Stone. I put it on the table next to her bed and suggested she read a few pages each night to help her sleep. At dinnertime, I lit candles and put her favorite music on. My attempt to ease her mind did not work. She tearfully shook her head and said, "Thanks, Giancarlo."

The week was the longest one I can remember. Neither of us slept very much the night before the operation. We arrived at the hospital an hour before our scheduled time. Gina was called, and a nurse dressed in surgery apparel introduced herself and greeted us. "Please come with me to prepare for the operation. Dr. Sullivan will see you before we move to the operating room."

I kissed Gina and hugged her and moved to the waiting room.

Four hours later, Dr. Sullivan walked out of the surgery room with a smile on his face and gave me the good news. "Gina did great, Mr. Giambrone. She is a champion. There is no doubt I got it all. The best news is it has not spread to her lymph glands. She will have a speedy recovery. I am going to have her do four weeks of radiation."

"Wow, Doctor, that is the best news I have heard in a long time. Thank you. Can I see her?"

"She is in the intensive care unit and will be out for a while. I gave her a sedative. Give it a couple of hours. The nurse will come and bring you to her."

I was getting impatient as a nurse came down the hall and asked, "Mr. Giambrone? Please come with me. I'll take you to your wife. She is awake and doing well."

We both shed a few tears when I entered the room. They were joyful tears as we embraced, and Gina said, "Thank God that is over."

"Are you in pain, Gina?"

"No, but the doctor told me I'm on painkiller medication that will last four hours, and later, the nurse will give me a pill to help me sleep. Have you been here all day? Did you eat anything?"

"I am fine. Don't worry about me. The nurse said I can sleep here on the couch tonight."

"That's silly, Giancarlo. Stay a little while and go home, eat something, and get some rest."

"No way. I'm staying."

I don't remember too much about the next three days. I felt like I was walking around in circles. I only left the hospital to go home, shower, and change clothes, occasionally stopping to grab a bite to eat.

Dr. Sullivan was in Gina's room when I walked in, and he had just examined her and given her the good news. "Gina, everything looks great. You may go home and eat some good Italian food. How does that sound?"

Gina's smile warmed my heart. I shook the doctor's hand and thanked him. I put on her robe and slippers and went to the main nurses' station and had a wheelchair brought into the room. On the way out, I stopped at the desk and paid the bill.

When we arrived at the house, the first thing out of her mouth was, "I want some pasta."

"Yes, ma'am. Relax. I'll have it on the table in twenty minutes"

After dinner, I went to the mailbox. I had not retrieved any mail for the five days while at the hospital. Gina said, "Will you please put the mail on your desk and come sit with me? It can wait another day."

We sat with little discussion. She ultimately fell asleep in my arms. When she woke up, I picked her up and carried her to bed.

*****

I received a letter from John Viviano. He had tried to call while Gina was in the hospital. Ponti Foods, one of his distributors, needed a large order of oil and was unable to secure it from Italy. It turned out he was successful getting it from a supplier in Spain, and we lost out on the opportunity. It also stated Evan Severino was interested in possibly working for Lucca Olive Oil after college. He was the young man we'd met on our visit a while back.

I phoned John and apologized for missing his call. He gave me the contact information for Ponti Foods, including the owner's name and phone number.

For Gina's four weeks of radiation, I was determined to be with her. While she had some discomfort after it, she never complained. The last treatment was on a Thursday, and we went to lunch at the club. Gina said, "We have not seen our friends for over a month. Why don't you call Sandra and Tom and Sharon and Tony and invite them to dinner here to celebrate the completion of my treatment?"

I made those calls when I got home and asked both Tom and Tony not to mention anything about the cancer.

We toasted Gina at dinner Saturday night. Both couples complied with my wish for no discussion about Gina's illness. Tom said, "So, Giancarlo, how is the olive oil business?"

I replied, "I have decided to sell it, Tom. I want to spend more time enjoying life with Gina."

Gina looked at me in shock. "Excuse me. What was that?" In a serious raised voice, she said, "You are not selling that business, Giancarlo. First of all, you have nothing to sell! You have a few distributors here and in Italy and a small business with a couple of restaurants and food stores. You are not a quitter. Quitters never win, and winners never quit."

Laughing, Tom said, "Well, Giancarlo, I guess that settles it. I'd suggest in the future, you discuss your plans for using the washroom with Gina before departing for it."

Even Gina laughed. It was great to be back to our normal life, dining with friends.

*****

I was looking forward to some leisure time reading and going to the movies. The movie about James Jones's book *From Here to Eternity* was finally released. It was about the bombing of Pearl Harbor in Hawaii by the Japanese, which caused President Roosevelt to declare war on Japan and have the US enter World War II.

There was a lot of controversy. The Legion of Decency, founded in 1932 by the Catholic church, initially banned it from being distributed to movie theaters, then more bad publicity over the fact that Frank Sinatra was initially denied the supporting role until some of his Italian friends intervened, and he got the part. But that rumor was never proven. Sinatra signed a contract for $8,000 and later was nominated for one of the eight Academy Awards the movie received.

The Legion of Decency was upset over the fact that Deborah Kerr and Burt Lancaster were having an adulterous affair, and the big concern was a scene where the two of them lay on the beach embracing and kissing in the moonlight. Over the objections, the movie was released and was a major success. This broke the ground for future sensual movies and ultimately ended the dominance of the Legion of Decency.

CHAPTER 7

Lucca
April 1953

I received a phone call from Evan Severino the morning we were leaving for Lucca. He asked to visit and interview for a job with us. I was a little surprised but liked his enthusiastic approach. He didn't mince any words about his work ethic nor about his experience in the food industry. I explained we were leaving for Lucca and suggested we get together later in the fall after he graduates from college.

He replied, "Mr. Giambrone, I graduate in August because I have one more class to finish. Is there any way we can finish this interview today, and if you agree to hire me, I can join your company at the end of August?"

I smiled and made the decision to bring him on. This was an aggressive kid. He reminded me of myself when I was twenty-two. "I'll tell you what, Evan. You are a good salesman, and I'm going to take a chance. Here's the plan: you are going to spend the end of August, September, and early October in Lucca. For a while, you will be in the field with the men preparing for the harvest of the ripe olives.

In September, depending on the summer heat, you'll be working nine- and ten-hour days, picking the olives and bringing them to the presses. You'll be sleeping in the dormitory with the men and eating with them. This is hard work six days a week. There's not much to do at night, but the men all go to town Saturday for fun and usually rest on Sundays.

Our cook is a gem. Her food is old Italian cuisine, and you'll never go to bed hungry."

"Mr. Giambrone, I am so excited about this opportunity, I can't wait to start."

"In early October, we will rendezvous in Rome and fly to Palm Springs, California. You'll begin training with me."

"What will be my duties?"

"You will be the liaison promoting our oil with specialty grocers like Viviano's and their sales reps. You'll also be calling on restaurants, convincing them to use olive oil for frying, and calling on our distributors."

I took a breath as Evan cut in, "Mr. Giambrone, I am so excited about this opportunity. I am eager to learn the business and travel!"

"Evan, I'm glad you want to travel. Later, you'll travel with me on a trip to interview new distributors. Once you have that experience, you'll be traveling on your own to search for new ones."

"Mr. Giambrone, I can bring in new business. I'm sure of it."

"I'm happy to hear you are so confident. Your starting pay for the last four months of this year will be twenty-five dollars a week. As of January 1954, you will earn fifty dollars a week plus travel and entertainment expenses. How does that sound?"

"Mr. Giambrone, I am so excited. I can barely get words out of my mouth. My only question is I have never been abroad. How do I get to Lucca?"

"I will have my travel agent contact you. Meanwhile, go to the post office and apply for a passport."

"Yes, Mr. Giambrone, right away."

"Congratulations, Evan. Welcome aboard."

"Mr. Giambrone, thank you from the bottom of my heart. I promise you will not regret this decision."

*****

Pleased with my phone call with Evan, I poured a cup of coffee and went out to the patio to watch the sunrise. It was a beautiful day to fly. Gina joined me and asked who was on the phone, and I shared the news about Evan. "Good move, Giancarlo. Now you need to move him to the West Coast and train him to handle the Western states and hire someone for the Midwest and the East Coast so that you can oversee the business."

"Yes, Boss, I just can't wait to get to Lucca and enjoy Anna's great meals."

"Hmm, I guess that makes my cooking secondary to hers. You have a unique way of moving into the doghouse, Giancarlo."

"Sorry, Gina, I did not infer that. Will you at least throw me a bone. How long will I be in the doghouse?"

"I have not set your sentence. I'll let you know when we arrive in Lucca."

Our flight was a breeze, and Salvatore was waiting for us in Firenze. On the way to the villa, I told him that Evan would be arriving late August. He was delighted to train him.

Upon arrival, I turned the TV on and learned that the US diplomats were making great progress negotiating the truce with North Korea and the Chinese. Those negotiations had been going on for nearly two years. On April 26, after seventeen days, an agreement was reached on a new agenda. Four main issues were on the table. They included a truce, a demilitarized zone to be established, a date for a ceasefire, and an armistice commission to oversee the issues.

Anna announced our dinner, and I opened a bottle of wine while Gina put on some of the latest records. They included Nat King Cole's latest, "Pretend"; "Vaya Con Dios" by Les Paul and Mary Ford; and followed by "Crying in the Chapel" by June Valli. I made sure not to mention the doghouse sentence nor a word about the incredible dinner Anna had prepared.

The next morning, we went into town to do some shopping. I bought the *Herald-Tribune* newspaper at the bookstore but did not see any books that interested me. We later stopped for coffee. "Gina, I want to go to Milan and meet with an advertising agency to create an ad campaign. I'm thinking of some ten- and twenty-second TV ads, showing a can or bottle with the logo and simple exposure of the brand name. For the States, I want to get an LA agency to create billboards."

"I like it, Giancarlo. Are you planning any other trips while we are here?"

"Well, I was reluctant to bring that up, but maybe a quick trip to visit our distributor in the Marche Region. They are located in Ancona. I have never been there. It is a historic old city. It would be the only other trip."

"Fine. Let's take a one-day trip back to Milan next week and spend the rest of the week in Ancona. Do you want me to go with you?"

"Well, I will be happy to have you join me, but unless you want to travel with me in the doghouse, it will not be possible"

"Giancarlo, do you know what happens to a smart-ass presently in the doghouse when he continues with asinine remarks?"

"No, but I am anxious to learn"

"He moves into a bigger doghouse with other dogs who have misbehaved. But in this case, because I love Milan, and I want to see Ancona, I will release you from captivity."

*****

We returned to the villa, and I moved to the balcony to read the newspaper. To my dismay, there was an extensive article about President Eisenhower increasing the arms supply to the French fighting in Vietnam. The US was even supplying the uniform's for them. Here we were trying to end the conflict in Korea and spending enormous sums of money for another war.

I turned the page to the business section and read about a new chain of roadside hotels called Holiday Inns. It was a franchise opportunity with plans to construct ten thousand units across the country to service the new interstate highway system President Eisenhower planned. The inns would have all-in-one service to attract families, with restaurants, swimming pools, and other features for extended stays.

For a break, we saw the movie *Stalag 17*, with William Holden. He had been nominated for an Academy Award for his portrayal of an army officer in a German prisoner camp in World War Il. It was a successful Broadway play based on a true story written by Donald Bevan and Ed Trzcinski, former German prisoners of war. The story opens with two prisoners attempting to escape, and both are shot. The officers begin to suspect there's a spy in the group who tipped off the Germans and later find their suspicions to be true. They plot the spy's demise, and they ultimately succeed. We enjoyed the action and pace of the movie.

On Monday the following week, we drove to Milan and met with an ad agency. Gina made a presentation with packaging and the brochure. At lunch, they made suggestions on airing regional TV commercials in areas where we had distribution. We concluded the meeting with a plan to return in a week or ten days to see some designs for approval. They asked that we work on a budget for the first year. Gina and I decided to see the volume of the fall harvest before we set the budget.

Later that week, we drove to Ancona. I had called for an appointment with our distributor and received a distant approval. It was a six-hour scenic drive, including a stop in Firenze for lunch. We checked in to a nice hotel and had some pasta for dinner in the hotel dining room.

We met with Giorgio Sanfillipo, our distributor in the area, the next morning. He blasted us for a good five minutes. The main complaint was he had not heard from anyone from our company in years. I allowed him to rant.

"Signore Sanfillipo, there are no words in my vocabulary to apologize for our lack of attention. The fact remains we are here. It was a six-hour drive from Lucca. I humbly ask, may we show you where Lucca Olive Oil is today?"

He nodded and said, "Proceed."

Gina was somewhat taken aback by his yelling, but being the trooper she is, she put the brochure on the table and showed no intimidation explaining it. She followed up with the packaging. I wasted no time discussing the price list, which I handed him. We were on a roll.

He looked at us with a smile and said, "I am sorry I yelled at you. The fact remains I have been buying my oil from a firm in Puglia. I like your packaging and the prices. I would like to taste the oil."

We put a bottle on the table. He produced a large spoon and poured some oil on it, and the smile on his face told the story. "It is good, Signore, real good, superior to that I buy from Puglia, but I can't buy any at this time. I have an exclusive contract with the firm in Puglia. However, it matures at the end of the year. I presume you will honor the same territory for all of the Marche Region I currently enjoy. Can you leave the sample of your oil?"

"Thank you, Signore Sanfillipo. The answer is yes to your questions. Will you honor us and join us for dinner tonight. Please have your wife join us at your favorite restaurant."

"That is nice of you to ask, and it will be on one condition Signore Giambrone. You are in my city, and dinner will be on me. No more discussion on the conto."

We dined at La Moretta, one of the oldest restaurants in Italy, and enjoyed meeting his wife, Maria. There was no discussion about the oil business. I started to ask the waiter if they fried with olive oil, but Gina kicked me under the table when I beckoned him. Instead, I asked him for a bottle of amarone wine.

The dinner was superb. We had pasta with a light cream sauce to start and a chicken breaded with house breadcrumbs and fried zucchini. Gina kicked me again when the zucchini arrived.

Signore Sanfilippo suggested a coffee shop in an old piazza in Ascoli Piceno just outside of Ancona. You must visit it in the morning. It has been in existence since the sixteenth century. He told us to make sure we have their homemade brioche. It is the best in Italy.

The next day was Sunday, and we went to the piazza and had the brioche with cappuccino. It was everything Signore Sanfillipo said it was. Gina bought two of the pastries to take back to Lucca. The drive home was flawless, thanks to the warm, sunny day.

*****

I received a call the following week from the ad agency in Milan. The storyboards were ready for our review and would be sent to us. We were both delighted when they arrived. There were four ten-second and four twenty-second spots to consider. We selected a twenty-second spot with our three-liter can with the caption, "Extra virgin olive oil from Tuscany, so pure you can fry with it, it's healthier." The ten-second spot showed our bottle with the same caption.

I put in a call to the agency with our selections. I told them I would submit the budget in October. The plan was to begin running the commercials for a test in Milan, Bologna, and Rome the third quarter of the year. I asked that they be aired on TV during the news hours at six o'clock and ten o'clock.

*****

I received a call from Giuseppe Sapienza, the owner of two small olive groves south of us near Pisa. They did not press the olives, so he sold the harvest each year. He offered the crop to us in the past, but we never had need for the extra olives. "Buon giorno, Giuseppe. What can I do for you?"

"Giancarlo, I have reached that age where I no longer want to be in the business, and I want to sell my land. Are you interested?"

"I might be, depending on the price and the yield. Why don't you prepare a five-year history of the annual production and a price and call me, and I'll drive down to discuss the proposition."

I discussed the call with Gina and received her usual conservative opinion. "Why would you want to add more stress to what you already have? It doesn't make sense, Giancarlo. Who is going to run the groves when Signore Sapienza retires? How do you guarantee the yield will be the same? What if the person harvesting sells off some of it to a former client that Sapienza was doing business with and the yield falls short? And at this time, do you need the extra olives? Please, Giancarlo, don't do it!"

"As usual, what you say makes sense. I will keep that in mind, but remember, our business is growing. We are limited to what we can produce, and that's it."

"Fine, Giancarlo, but when that period arrives, why not buy the harvest from whoever makes the deal with Sapienza. Why buy the cow when you can just buy the milk?"

"Come here and hug me, Ms. Aristotle. You are such a philosopher. I always knew there was a hidden reason I married you."

"Were there other reasons? Be quick, junior. Don't take too much time to think. You're about to start digging the proverbial hole."

"Gee, Gina, there are so many. I don't know where to start—at least a hundred."

"That works. Quick thinking—you dodged a bullet."

"I am still going to listen. I want to know the yield in case we need the production in the future."

After listening to Signore Sapienza's proposition the following week, I told him at this time, I did not need the extra supply and wished him the best in the sale and his future retirement.

Siracusa
July

We arrived at our haven in Sicily in a major rainstorm. It was rare. Sicily's annual rainfall was about the same as that in the desert for Palm Springs. Vincenzo picked us and drove us to the villa. Alena greeted us warmly and informed us dinner would be ready shortly.

I opened a bottle of wine, put some music on the record player, and asked Gina what she planned for the ensuing weeks. "I would like to go to Malta. The history of that country is amazing, and perhaps while we are there, you can inquire about their use of olive oil."

"Good idea. You're starting to think like a real entrepreneur."

"Thanks. I have a good teacher."

We enjoyed a great dinner, and afterward, Gina said, "Why do we ever go out to dinner here or in Lucca? The food is better here."

I said, "I feel the same when we are in Palm Springs. Your cooking is better than the restaurants there."

"Is that a compliment with a string because we will soon be calling it a night? Are you expecting a reward?"

"I refuse to answer on the grounds I might be incriminating myself."

After breakfast the next morning, we drove into town and stopped by the travel agency and booked the trip to Malta for the following week. We were given a brochure on its history, which we both read while having a cappuccino at the local café. Gina handed it to me after scanning it. "Here, Giancarlo, I have read about most of this."

Malta and the Maltese islands had been occupied six thousand years before Christ was born. It had been inhabited early by Sicilians in 5900 BC, and some of the ruins of their temples survived. The Phoenicians arrived and took control in 800 BC, followed by Carthage in 600 BC. When Rome conquered Sicily in 250 BC, Malta fell under their rule. Eventually, the Arabs, Normans, and the knights ruled. In the eighteenth century, France became the new leader.

The brochure described the culture, language, and architecture of all those rulers can be seen in the country today. Because it was aligned with Italy during World War II, it was heavily bombed. After the war, it fell under the rule of the British Empire and only recently reached independence.

The boat trip to Malta was wonderful. We spent the entire trip on deck and enjoyed the warm weather. The bright sun glistened on the calm ocean, and the sea breeze kept the heat comfortable.

The travel agent did a great job making our hotel selection, and we checked in to the honeymoon suite at the Xara Palace. The minute we walked into the room, Gina's needle surfaced. "So, handsome, tell me. Did you bribe the man at the travel agency to reserve this suite with mischievous intentions?"

"I'm sorry. I didn't hear you."

"You heard me, devil."

We decided to take a walk after we unpacked and found the area around the hotel charming. There were many exclusive shops and fine restaurants, and we had a delightful lunch. For dinner that first evening, our agent in Siracusa again selected a famed age-old restaurant, Caffe Condina, founded in 1837. The food lived up to its success and enabled their survival all those years.

I waited until we had finished dinner and asked to see the manager. When he arrived, he asked if there was a problem. I introduced Gina and myself and explained we were from Siracusa, and we were in the olive oil business. Gina put our brochure on the table. I spoke briefly about the quality of our oil and asked who their oil supplier was. "Thank you for your information, Mr. Giambrone. We are supplied by a purveyor from Sicily, and all the oil is Sicilian."

I got the kick under the table from Gina, thanked him, and requested the check.

We spent the next two days with suggestions from the island brochure, including a walking tour of the city of Valletta. It included some of the finer buildings of the city. We visited several temples that dated back three thousand years before the birth of Christ. We concluded the sightseeing with a visit to Medina, the antiquated former capital of Malta. The lucrative past was exemplified in the opulent palaces and baroque architecture.

Our sail back to Siracusa was as pleasant as our trip over. The rest of our stay in Siracusa was joyous. The best part was the truce ending the war in Korea. The sad news were the statistics—23,613 Americans died, the casualties numbered 36,516, and there were 4,817 missing in action. The total financial cost was not disclosed.

There was more bad news coming out of Vietnam. The French were getting whipped on all fronts by the North Vietnamese military and taking on major losses. Ho Chi Minh, the leader of the communist forces in North Vietnam, was determined to gain independence from French domination, which had basically enslaved the people of Vietnam since 1850.

*****

October

We stopped in Rome for a day to visit our distributor Signore Pelligrino. He was delighted to see us. We had lunch, and he informed us our oil was doing well both in the stores and restaurants. His sales help followed our procedures in selling the restaurants on the idea of frying with oil as opposed to lard, and they were winning the battle. He handed me a reorder just before our food arrived.

Evan Severino joined us at the airport in Rome the next morning for our flight to New York. He was delighted with his time in Lucca and anxious to begin the next phase of his training.

November

We arrived in LA with Evan the first week of November and brought him to our home in Palm Springs for two days. I called John Viviano in St. Louis and asked him to make arrangements to meet with the distributor he had told me about. He returned my call a few hours later and said we could meet the following Monday.

Evan and I flew to St. Louis Sunday afternoon, and his younger brother Brock picked us up. They dropped me off at the Chase Hotel, and Evan went to stay with his family.

On Monday, we went to Angelo's for lunch with John Viviano and John Ferrara, one of the owners of Ponti Food and Cheese Distribution. After lunch, I presented the brochure, packaging, and pricing. Angelo fried all the food for lunch in our olive oil. He even put a small saucer of the oil on the table for us to dip our bread.

John Ferrara explained his business and that his firm had recently purchased the largest cheese distributor in the area. He also mentioned he imports canned tomatoes from Italy. I asked what states he covered, and he replied, "We cover Missouri, Kansas, and Oklahoma."

"That's perfect, John. We do not have distribution in those states. I brought our five-year contract with us with conservative annual volume increases. It includes a five-year option. I'd like for you to take it with you and get back to us in the next twenty-four hours, if possible, to sign it before we leave. Please feel free to take more time if you need to review it with your attorney. We leave Wednesday for the East Coast."

"Giancarlo, why don't we plan to have dinner here tomorrow night to sign it?"

We signed the agreement Tuesday night before dinner. John had a bottle of champagne on ice next to our table, and we toasted each other. He showed additional class when the bill arrived by paying for dinner, and the added plus was a sizable order for cans and bottles. He left, but I asked Evan to sit for a while. "So, Evan, what do you think?"

"Well Mr. Giambrone, seems to me he was presold before we sat down for lunch. Maybe I am not reading between the lines. It looks easy."

I smiled and said, "You are forgetting the day we met, and the groundwork with your old boss, convincing him to join Gina and me for dinner at Angelo's and then impressing him and Angelo to fry with our oil."

"Yes, I remember you told me about that meeting."

"There's another lesson. John Ferrara's former supplier let him down and failed to deliver the large order he had placed. Bear in mind Evan, we have good oil, better than most, but there is competition. In the final analysis, all we have to sell is service. That's where you will come in. I want you to move to California and call on restaurants and specialty-food stores to help our distributor build the business. My plan is to have three of you doing that, with one here in the Midwest and, ultimately, one on the East Coast."

"I'm ready to move and do whatever you need me to do, Mr. Giambrone."

"Good. So from now on, please call me Giancarlo."

"That will take a while for me to get used to."

We flew to New York the next morning and began calling on restaurants in Little Italy. We heard the same answers in all the restaurants in all five boroughs. "We don't fry with olive oil."

In more than one, we heard, "You don't want to know who we purchase our oil from."

Another obnoxious reply from a person in a fine Italian restaurant was, "Why do you need to know who sells us our oil?"

After two days of lunches and dinners, it was obvious the distribution was controlled by the mob. We decided to fly to Boston to try our luck. We checked in to the Ritz-Carlton and immediately went to the Italian neighborhood called North End, also known as Little Italy. I had the concierge make lunch and dinner reservations for the next two days.

We dined at three restaurants, Cantina Italiana, Régine Pizzeria, and Union Oyster House and, as usual, got the same reply: "We use lard for frying. Olive oil is too expensive."

We had the pleasure of showing our oil to managers and/or assistant managers at all three, and they loved the taste of the oil. There was a common answer as to whom they used for purveyors: Italo/America Purveyors of Italian Food and Cheese. We secured a contact and phone number. The owner was Ricardo Pozzini.

The next morning, I made a call to Mr. Pozzini, and he agreed to see us in the afternoon. I called Evan's room, and there was no answer. After I showered and dressed, I knocked on his door. He opened the door in his underwear and apologized for oversleeping.

He sheepishly came down for breakfast later and again apologized for his tardiness. I waited until he was served with coffee and gave him his first lesson on Giambrone philosophy. "Evan, punctuality is the option of kings. If you tell someone you will meet at a certain time, you be damn sure you are there fifteen minutes early. Do you understand? When you are late, you have wasted the other person's time. When you are on the road and in a hotel, get in the habit of leaving a wake-up call with the hotel operator with a second call a few minutes later."

"Yes, sir, Mr. Giambrone. I promise it will not happen again."

Our meeting went well with Mr. Pozzini. He gave us a test order and promised if he had success, he would introduce us to his distributor on our next trip.

Gina picked us up at the airport in LA. She had researched apartments, and we found one for Evan. It was a nice one-room efficiency in a neighborhood close to many shops. I made arrangements to meet him in a couple days to start making calls on our purveyors and restaurants using our oil and to meet our distributor Sam Marzullo.

When Gina and I arrived in Palm Springs, I made calls and set up appointments for the coming week. Gina cooked a nice dinner while I watched the news on TV, and after dinner, I shared experiences regarding our trip.

The following week, I brought Evan one of my old briefcases, brochures, samples of cans and bottles, and price lists. We spent three days calling on our existing clients and concluded with lunch with Sam Marzullo. He had some interesting suggestions for Evan. They included restaurants and purveyors to contact who had not climbed on our oil bandwagon. These were Sam's clients scattered across the entire state of California.

After lunch, I took Evan to Bank of America and gave him an advance, and he opened a checking account. I then made arrangements for him to have a car in California.

December

Gina invited Tom and Sandra to spend the Christmas and New Year holidays with us. They arrived on the twenty-third just in time for dinner.

After breakfast, Tom and I drove to the Chevrolet dealer in town and picked up a new 1954 Corvette I had ordered for Gina for Christmas. Tom was in awe of it. We test-drove it, and then I paid the dealer, and we drove back to the house. Tom rang the doorbell, and Gina answered with a surprised look on her face. I was sitting in the Corvette, and she could not believe her eyes. She approached me and said, "You did not tell me you were buying yourself a new car. You just bought your Mercedes last year."

I got out of the car, put my arm around her, and said, "This is all you get for Christmas."

I received the best hug since our wedding night.

Soon, Sandra, hearing all the commotion, came out and saw the car. She looked at Tom and said, "Well, Tom, I assume you have a plan to put smiles on my face when we get back to Laguna."

Tom was quick to reply, "Mrs. Venegoni, remember, we are on a fixed income. I am not a big olive-oil tycoon."

With that, we all went inside to plan our end-of-year holiday together. We celebrated New Year's Eve with Sharon and Tony and welcomed 1954.

CHAPTER 8

Palm Springs
January 1954

We received a cable from Salvatore Vitale. One of his key people resigned, and he requested permission to hire his brother Giuseppe. He stated his brother was willing to work for the same pay; therefore, there would be no increase in overhead. I sent a quick reply, approving the move.

Gina called an ad agency in LA for an appointment. We put some ideas together for the billboard campaign for three cities: San Diego, Los Angeles, and San Francisco. She created sketches prior to the meeting, and they were very well received. Included was a twenty-foot-by-thirty-foot board, with part of the can extended from the top. The designer at the studio loved it but cautioned that the board would have to be custom-built, and there would be an upcharge. I asked for a quote and an estimate to run in all three cities for six months.

We also discussed designing some copy for newspaper ads in various sizes. These would be supplied to specialty stores in conjunction with a co-op advertising plan I had developed. The cost of the ad would be shared by the store and us, each paying 50 percent of the cost.

I received a call from US customs the day we returned, requesting a meeting regarding an illegal shipment of olive oil at the Long Beach, California, docks. Customs seized the container because it arrived with false documents. I agreed to meet the agents.

They had several bottles and cans in their office, and we opened them both. The were labeled, "Extra, Extra, virgin olive oil."

I explained to the agent, "First of all, there is no such thing as extra, extra virgin olive oil."

Next it was obvious that the oil had been diluted with water. It was thin and light. The label said, "Made in Italy," but the documents showed the country of origin was Spain. My recommendation was to target the receiving firm and investigate. This was a serious scam, trying to sell bad olive oil. My concern was twofold. First, it could cast a bad reputation on olive oil by people who would purchase it at any level—restaurants, grocers, and the ultimate consumer. My second concern was if they continued to import it, it could be harmful to our legitimate olive oil coming into the country by underselling us pricewise.

I left, confident that customs would arrest the culprits and end any threat. I planned to discuss the matter with the authorities for product control in Milan on my next trip.

February

Gina and I decided to have dinner at the country club to celebrate my birthday. Sandra and Tom, along with Sharon and Tony, surprised me by joining us. Separate conversations were happening. The three ladies were engaged in one on their own. Tom and Tony were in a debate about baseball, and my mind was drifting back to the day in the '20s when I met Tom and Sandra. I had begun working as an intern in the brokers office where Tom was employed. He took me under his wing and guided me. Soon, the business relationship led to friendship with him and Sandra. My marriage to Gina enhanced it.

Sharon and Tony rounded out the group. We met at the country club in Palm Springs. Everything revolved around the impact they had on my life. I was grateful for the friendships.

I beckoned to the waiter to bring us a bottle of champagne. I celebrated my fifty-fourth birthday feeling more grateful than ever.

We returned to the ad agency and reviewed their interpretation of the billboard design and the costs of the six-month program and approved it. We also liked the newspaper ad layouts and approved them. We got multiple copies of the news layouts to distribute to clients who wished to participate in the co-op program.

April

We arrived in Lucca to dry weather. It had not rained the entire spring. Salvatore came to see me the first day and expressed concern. He informed me there had been very little snow during the winter, and he was fearful of a possible long-term drought. I put his mind at ease. "Salvatore, we can't control the weather, so all we can do is wait."

I thought back to my college days at U of Bologna and Emerson's great quote: "What fears we've endured that failed to arrive." I shared it with Salvatore and told him to relax.

It was unusually hot in April, and the heat continued into May. I consulted with Salvatore, and he related that his men were trimming the dead branches from the trees. This would result in a reduced crop, which would lower our yield. I told him that we would buy olives from the two groves south of us if needed.

I placed a call to Signore Sapienza, who owned those groves, and learned he had not sold the property. He, too, was enduring the drought but said he would be happy to accommodate us.

Gina and I had discussed the drought and agreed not to allow it to affect our time in Lucca. We enjoyed going into the city center to shop and to see movies. We saw *On the Waterfront* with Marlon Brando and *The Country Girl* with Grace Kelly.

Our music was getting stale, and we decided to buy a few new records. Black musicians and singers were *Billboard* magazine's top hits. We bought Roy Hamilton's *You'll Never Walk Alone*, "Shake, Rattle and Roll" by Big Joe Turner, "Sh-Boom" by the Chords, and "Ebb Tide" by Roy Hamilton.

May

On the seventh of May, while watching the news, I was not surprised to learn the French military had suffered a major defeat at their garrison at Dien Bien Phu. It supposedly had been their last chance to defeat the North Vietnamese Army. Their decision to walk away from Vietnam was no surprise. I had told Gina and our friends it was inevitable. There was no question President Eisenhower had no choice but to get us into that conflict.

June

We were awakened in the middle of the night by severe thunder and lightning, followed by a monster rainstorm that continued until late morning. This was no ordinary storm; it was a monsoon. I could see Salvatore smiling and thought about the impact the weather has on our lives. That rain had no apparent effect on most of the people in the area, but it had an emotional and financial effect on the farmers. It brought a smile on our faces, and I am sure it had the same feeling for Salvatore.

Gina and I had not discussed the oil business very much since our arrival. Between the drought, movies, some reading, and the TV, we were distracted. "So, Giancarlo, what's on your mind these days about the olive oil business?"

"Well, we will not know the results of the drought until the fall harvest. I have been thinking of hiring someone for the Midwest to follow the path Evan is doing in California. His younger brother Brock will be graduating this month. I'm going to have him train here in July and remain through harvest, then I'll have him return to California to train with Evan. I'll work with him when we return from Italy. We need distributors in Atlanta and Dallas to complete our distribution network across the country."

I sent a cable to Evan, stating I had made the decision to hire Brock. I also met with Salvatore regarding Brock, and he promised he would take good care of the kid.

The weather gods continued to bless us with rain throughout the month of June. There was no question the drought had ended.

Gina and I had a discussion regarding my plans once the distributors were established across the country. I said, "The healthy use of olive oil for other products, such as soap and cosmetics, is our next

venture. Why don't we take a trip to Milan and make some cold calls on cosmetics and soap firms?"

"I like it, Giancarlo. It's the age-old story: 'build a better mousetrap.'"

"Once again, Ms. Aristotle, you have surprised me with your wisdom."

"Careful. There's a large pothole you're approaching, and you left your trendy shovel at home."

"Seriously, Gina, please work your magic and make reservations for three nights in Milan for the hotel and dinners, and I'll make some calls to find some manufactures for us to call on."

The next morning, I placed a call to the economic development office in Milan and got several factory names and made several appointments for us. We drove to Milan in a blinding rainstorm, but the bright sun was shining as we approached the city center. We had dinner at the hotel and called it a night.

Our appointment the next morning was with the marketing department and a scientist at the Accardi Soap Company. We brought a three-liter can of oil for them to test. The scientist was really interested in the potential. He told us his grandmother used olive oil to wash her face at night, and she lightly moisturized her face and hands with it. Her skin was as smooth as silk into her late eighties. This sparked sincere interest by the head of marketing. He asked, "Are you seeing any other soap companies while in Milan?"

I said, "Not after this presentation. Our goal is work with one firm in each category for extended use of our oil and back them in launching their product."

Our next appointment was with La vie en Rose Cosmetics. Again, we asked both marketing and a scientist to attend the presentation. Gina opened the meeting, stressing the health qualities of olive oil. She wasted no time relating to the meeting the day before at the soap company, and the scientist's line about his grandmother's use of oil. This raised smiles on the faces of both gentlemen in the meeting. We discussed various uses for their cosmetics. I agreed to be involved in marketing any product they would produce should they choose to use our oil.

There was serious interest on their part. They asked us to leave the three-liter can, and they also asked if we were seeing any of their competitors. I quickly said no. They were pleased with that answer.

This time, our return drive through the beautiful Lombardy countryside was beautiful. We stopped in Pavia for lunch on the way and made note of the tiny trattoria for the next time we were in the area. I was optimistic about the soap-and-cosmetic possibilities for our oil.

CHAPTER 9

Siracusa
July 1954

I received a cable from Evan, stating Brock was on board and would be traveling to Lucca once he graduated from Ole Miss University. He was excited and thanked me for the opportunity. Evan added, "You have my heartfelt thanks too, Mr. Giambrone. We are grateful for your confidence in us."

Gina and I went to town for coffee, and I bought the *Herald-Tribune* back copies for the past week, and we both read a little at the café. The business section had an interesting article about Boeing's recent launch of their mighty 707 jet airplane. It could carry up to 189 passengers. This was a first, and it substantially reduced the cost for international fares and made travel abroad more affordable for a broader consumer base.

Gina and I discussed how economical this could be for countries all over the world, especially for Europe. European agricultural revival was doing well after the ravages of World War II. Wine production also was helping the surge for the economy in Italy, as was their apparel business. Efforts were undertaken to restore historical landmarks throughout Italy. There was a rush for a cultural restoration too. It seemed like they were preparing for the increase in tourism with the advent of the Boeing 707.

The business section also announced the arrival of the first German Volkswagens in the US automobile market, and it met with mixed emotions, especially in the city of Detroit. Negative sentiment against anything made in Germany and Japan had not ceased since the end of World War II.

The war news in Vietnam was not good. North Vietnam's guerrilla army was making major advances toward the south, and they had established supply stations in Laos and Cambodia, with supplies entering from the USSR and China. I told Gina how ridiculous this was in as much as we just ended a conflict with China last year. President Eisenhower's answer was sending US Army advisors to assist and train South Vietnamese officers. He feared if Vietnam fell to communism, there would be a domino effect throughout Southeast Asia.

In other news, the US Supreme Court found segregation in US schools unconstitutional. I looked at Gina and said, "I don't know why I bought these newspapers. There's no good news. But times are changing regarding segregation and the integration of blacks in all facets of our culture."

We drove back to the villa and welcomed the beautiful warm ocean breezes. Gina put on some nice Mantovani instrumental music. I opened a bottle of wine, and we enjoyed the fruits of Alena's fine cuisine on the patio. There was no discussion about the morning's negative news.

"I have some plans I'd like to discuss with you about our business here in Italy. What do you think of promoting Salvatore and having him assume the responsibility for sales and marketing here. He graduated from the University of Milan with a degree in teaching. He could not find a job teaching after the war because Italy's economy was a disaster, so he ended up working for us. He's smart, knows the olive oil business, has a pleasant personality, and I know I can train him. He has what it takes to build relationships with our distributors. Now that we have covered Italy with distributors throughout the country, we need to support them with service if we want to increase the volume. Too often, they run out of product completely or run low on items, and someone needs to be checking their stock periodically for reorders. What do you think?"

"I love it, Giancarlo. It will also allow us to come to Italy and resume our original plan to enjoy the fruits of your labor without the stress of the work Salvatore will be doing."

"Fruits of our labor, Mrs. Giambrone.

When we return next April, I will take a few trips with him to visit the distributors. Meanwhile I am going to call him and explore his thoughts about the idea. I want him to begin training his brother Giuseppe to take his position. This will give Salvatore nine months to get Giuseppe ready.

I made the call to Salvatore the next morning. Fortunately, he was in the office. He was stunned and initially speechless. He said, "Signore, I am honored. I don't know what to say. The first problem is I have never sold anything. I have limited travel experience, and I don't have the proper clothes or shoes, and my car is an old Fiat from the '30s."

"Salvatore, these are simple things that money can fix. Let's take these negatives one at a time. We will buy you a used late-model company car. I personally will go with you to the city center in Lucca for the clothes you'll need.

As to selling, it's knowing your product and communicating that knowledge to the buyer. Who knows our oil better than you? As for traveling, I will accompany you on a few trips and make introductions to our distributors. You'll get the hang of it after those trips. Now let's talk about money."

"Signore Giambrone, please, whatever you decide is fine. I trust you."

"No, Salvatore, I want you to have incentive to travel and build the business. There will be a salary and commission and travel expenses. Let me have a few days to come up with a plan for us to discuss the next time we speak.

What do you think of asking your brother Giuseppe to take your place?"

"I love it, and he will be gratified. When do you want to start this plan, Signore Giambrone?"

"Salvatore, please start calling me Giancarlo. Signore Giambrone was my father. I want you to start training Giuseppe immediately. You will have until next April to train him. When we arrive, you and I will start traveling to meet our distributors. One thing to keep in mind: you have to be there next September for the harvest and for pressing the olives."

"Signore...excuse me, Giancarlo, this is a blessing I never dreamed of. I have always felt my future was following the footsteps of Giuseppe Fragale, spending the rest of my life in the field. You know my work ethic. Believe me, that work ethic will carry forward in my new position."

"I have no doubt, Salvatore—none whatsoever. Congratulations, my friend."

*****

In my perusing of the news in the States, I learned that the supreme court case regarding segregation was causing major problems in the South. It began when a man in Topeka, Kansas, filed a lawsuit against the public-school system because his daughter was not allowed to enter elementary school solely based on the color of her skin. He won the case, and she was admitted.

In the Deep South, segregationists organized and revolted against the supreme court decision. They caused massive resistance, forcing delays in allowing the rule to be implemented. Fights ensued against protesters in their attempts to push through desegregation.

During the riots, shots were fired into the crowds. Black churches were bombed. Economic intimidation became prevalent against black-owned businesses. Liberal whites marching with the black protesters were targeted and harmed. This brought global attention through television. Racial segregation was no longer a secret in America as it had been for 250 years. Race riots became the daily news item on TV.

I told Gina that it was not going to get resolved overnight. The South has been fighting the civil war since 1860, and this was not just another skirmish; it was a serious uprising.

October

Our time in Siracusa was drawing to a close. We were both eager to return to Palm Springs, to join our friends, and the warm sunshine of the desert. For me, there was continued work building the business. Boredom had seeped into the slow-paced life at our haven by the sea. I sensed Gina was getting a little bored too.

I called Marco Pelligrino, our distributor in Rome, and made a dinner date with him. Gina presented the storyboards regarding our

TV campaign, and he lit up like a Christmas tree. "Gina and Giancarlo, this is amazing. There is no doubt it will spark our sales. May I suggest when you go to the next level, create a commercial with a woman frying with the oil. It doesn't need any dialogue. All that's needed is her dropping a few drops of oil from a bottle with the logo in a pan and adding a slice of meat or a vegetable to the pan to send the message."

I made a mental note of the suggestion. He said he was planning a trip to Lucca in April to visit us and handed me a nice reorder as we departed. I thanked him for his business, and we said our goodbyes.

We flew Pan American Airways's new jet service to New York and also to LA. The food and overall accommodations were amazing. International travel had come a long way since spending ten to fourteen days at sea, long hours on trains, and the drives to reach our villas.

Sandra and Tom Venegoni picked us up and drove us to Palm Springs, a joyous reunion with our close friends.

*****

November

The beautiful desert weather allowed Tom and me to enjoy golf and time together, and I welcomed the camaraderie. Sandra and Gina shared the same togetherness. It dawned on me that we had no serious friendships in Italy, which made our friendships here all the more special.

I placed a call to Evan Severino, and we discussed his experiences while we were away. We had a lengthy discussion about his brother Brock, and he reported Brock was learning fast. "Giancarlo, Brock is ready to begin the second phase of his training with you and calling on new distributor prospects. Do you have any specific plans? He is getting anxious."

"As a matter of fact, I have plans to visit Atlanta, Dallas, and Boston to complete our distribution network, and he will be traveling with me. Once we have established those three areas, I intend to relocate him to Chicago or St. Louis so he can take on the same responsibility you have."

"Great, Giancarlo. He'll be happy to hear that. By the way, while Brock was in Lucca, he became concerned about one of the field workers who got involved with a woman in town. Brock heard she had been a prostitute during the war, and he feels she was taking advantage of him."

"Do you know the name of the worker?"

"No, but I'll ask my brother and get back to you."

I hung up the phone, making a mental note to follow up on this news. I did not want our oil business negatively affected by a field worker's dalliance.

Sharon and Tony invited us to their home in Beverly Hills for Thanksgiving. Gina was delighted she didn't have to cook. During the weekend, we saw a preview of the movie *Marty* with Ernest Borgnine. The acting by Borgnine and his costar Betsy Blair was great, but it was depressing at first. Marty was an aging Italian bachelor and a butcher. He lived with his mother and rarely ventured out into the real world. And then one night, urged by his mom, he went to the Stardust Dance Ballroom, and he met a lonely school teacher, Clara (Betsy Blair), and began a courtship. His family tried to discourage him from pursuing the romance. He had to decide between their approval of him or continuing the relationship. In the end, he tells his friends he is going to get down on his knees and beg her to marry him.

When we left the theater, I said to Gina, "Thank you for rescuing me when you did. There are many lonely people in the world with Marty's experience before he met Clara. Most are not blessed the way he was. Their lonely lives never cease to end. I could have been one of those lonely hearts if you had not come along."

Gina, laughing, said, "Get serious, Giancarlo. With your looks, your personality, and your line of BS, that never would have happened, but thanks for the compliment."

We returned to the desert and resumed our regular routines of golf and tennis. I received a phone call from Ricardo Pozzini, the purveyor we met in Boston. He informed me he decided to become a food-and-wine distributor. "Giancarlo, I am importing canned tomatoes from San Marzano. Prosciutto, salami, and Parmigiano cheese from Parma. And Asiago cheese from the Veneto Region. I would like to be your distributor in New England if you'll have me."

"Great news, Ricardo. As a matter of fact, I was planning a trip to Boston after the first of the year with my new salesman. How are you on the tenth of January?"

"I'm at your disposal, Giancarlo."

"I'll see you later that afternoon. Thanks for the call."

*****

Sandra and Tom invited us to spend the Christmas and New Year holidays with them at their home in Laguna Beach. It was a nice escape from the desert heat. It was extremely hot when we left, and we welcomed the cool evening breezes from the Pacific.

Sharon and Tony joined us on New Year's Eve, and we ushered in 1955. Tony had a surprise for us on New Year's Day. Our California distributor Sam Marzullo invited us to spend the day on his yacht, and once on board, Sandra said, "This is living the dream."

Yes, we were living the dream.

Salvatore Vitale

Left to right: Sam Marzullo and his wife Nancy, Sandra and Tom Venegoni, Giancarlo and Gina, and Sharon and Tony Bomaritto.

CHAPTER 10

Palm Springs
January 1955

The new year held some real excitement regarding the oil business, and I was eager to get back to it. I called Evan and discussed the past three months' activities in California. Then I spoke to Brock regarding the name of the field worker and the woman Brock had mentioned with concern earlier. "Signore Giambrone, his name is Marco Fellugo, and her name is Veronica Bartolino. I only met her once. I did not spend a lot of time with them. There's no doubt he is smitten. He was buying her clothing and other expensive gifts."

"Thanks, Brock. I am worried that Marco may divulge the techniques we are using to achieve the quality of our oil. Our specially designed filtration equipment is second to none. The method we use allows the paste to warm after pressing, and the separation process is another proprietary procedure we developed. Our method results in a more pure extra virgin oil. The time we allow for separation of the liquids is different from other producers. They rush the process, and that's why our oil is superior to theirs."

Brock replied, "I, too, am concerned about Marco. He is a nice man and a hard worker. He keeps to himself, so I did not get to know him. I am sure he is lonely, and she has wooed him. She is very attractive, and the other men have teased him. I feel sorry for him. Hope this turns out to be of no concern."

"Brock, I understand your concern, and I know you'll keep on this. Meanwhile, you and I are flying to Boston on the tenth. Do you have a suit and tie?"

"I do, Signore. I am ready to learn as much as I can with you. My experience in Lucca was incredible. If people only knew what it takes to make a bottle of olive oil. They would never complain about the price. More significantly, Anna's frying with it was amazing.

"There's another thing I do not understand. It's so much healthier compared to frying with lard. They are putting food in their stomachs and are concerned about the expense. Most of them smoke, and they think nothing of inhaling nicotine."

"Wow, Brock, keep thinking that way, and be sure to convey that message when we are talking to our new distributor. You just gave me several ideas to share with our purveyors and distributors."

I shared the news about the field worker with Gina. "Why are you so calm, Giancarlo? Don't you want to investigate what's going with that guy and his girlfriend? How much does he earn? Where's the money coming from for him to buy her expensive gifts?"

"Gina, your suspicious mind is getting you upset without knowing anything about the situation. He earns the equivalent of twenty dollars a week plus room and board. He works six days a week. So he has nowhere to spend his money. Let's see what an investigation shows."

"Giancarlo, please send a cable right now to Salvatore and ask him to investigate. He should have the man in the office with a police officer there to intimidate him. They need to discover what information he has shared with her about the processes used during harvest and pressing."

"Yes, I have already talked to Brock about this, but I will send a cable as you suggest."

Brock and I flew to Boston and checked in to the Ritz-Carlton. We met Ricardo Pozzini for dinner, and I introduced Brock. We discussed the distribution agreement at length. Signore Pozzini showed us his plan for marketing our oil in New England and Maine and requested samples to accommodate his three sales people.

Brock wasted no time getting into the conversation and used the same selling features he had discussed with me. Ricardo looked at him and said, "How old are you, son? That was impressive. Would you be willing to spend a few days and train my salesmen while you're here?"

I interrupted, "Ricardo, let's have a sales meeting. Can we do it at our hotel tomorrow morning?"

"Absolutely, Giancarlo. Let's sign the contract. I'm anxious to get started."

The next day, we held the sales meeting with Ricardo's team. I allowed Brock to make the presentation, and it was perfect. I was impressed, as was Ricardo, who later complimented him.

We flew back to California. I informed Brock we'd be flying to Atlanta the following week, with a stopover in St. Louis and Chicago. I shared our success with Gina. "Wow, Giancarlo, another piece of the puzzle. All that's left is Atlanta and Dallas."

"Right, Gina. Brock and I will be heading there next week."

Laughing, she said, "I'm sure I can find something to do to keep my mind occupied for a couple of days while you wander off into the sunset. Do you remember we live together sir?"

"Sorry, Gina, but it will be more than a couple of days. We are stopping in St. Louis and Chicago. I want Brock to meet our distributors there. I was planning on having you join us."

"That invitation, Mr. Giambrone, saved you from the deepest hole in our marital history. You had one foot in it and one on the banana peel. I'll make plane, hotel reservations, and dining plans for all the cities. Shall I plan two days in Atlanta and Dallas?"

"Please do, boss. Thanks. You never let up from keeping me on my toes. I truly believe you enjoy inserting your needle in the most sensitive part of my brain."

Gina began preparing dinner. I put some new records on the record player. I had no idea who the singers were. The first was by a group called Bill Haley & His Comets. When it began, I could not believe my ears. It was raucous. The title said it all: "Rock around the Clock." Gina came running into the den when she heard it. I laughed and said, "Where did you hear about this guy?"

She replied, "It's the latest rage among the kids. It's called rock and roll."

"Gina, may I remind you we are no longer teenagers."

"Giancarlo, I'm desperately holding back the big hand and the little hand on the clock with both my arms and legs. I have no intention to grow old gracefully, and my goal is to follow the same procedure with you."

To humor her, I allowed the record to finish, then I put on some easy listening tunes. The Platters had a new one, "The Great Pretender." Next was Count Basie and Joe Williams's rendition of "Every Day I Have the Blues."

Gina mentioned she bought new books for us to read. "They are on your desk, Giancarlo. I bought *The Man in the Gray Flannel Suit* by Sloan Wilson—I have never heard of him—and John O'Hara's latest, *Ten North Frederick*, which is on the *New York Times*'s bestseller list."

Gina knew my taste in books, so I looked forward to reading them.

*****

We flew to St. Louis. Gina and I checked in to the Chase Hotel. Brock stayed with his parents. We agreed to meet the next day at Sala's for lunch with John Viviano and John Ferrara from Ponti Foods.

Gina and I had dinner at Tony's. Vince Bomaritto greeted us warmly and brought us to our table. The waiter brought warm bread and a small dish of our oil to the table. We looked at Vince and smiled. He smiled too. The dinner presentation was a creative masterpiece. Two cannelloni served with a cream sauce so delicate, that it left no question it was slowly reduced sans any flour. It was so picturesque. We were reluctant to take that first bite. The second course was a boneless, skinless sliced chicken breast so tender, there was no need for a knife. I was thrilled to have such a fine restaurant using our oil.

At the meeting the next day, I introduced Brock to John Ferrara, and John Viviano gave him a warm hug. "Mr. Ferrara, Brock will eventually be acting as liaison working with you and your purveyors. He will make calls on both existing clients and new prospects with your sales people."

John Ferrara asked, "When will Brock begin the new program?"

I replied, "Sometime in the next sixty days."

Gina presented a photo of the billboard we planned to run in California and explained if successful, our goal was to run it next in the Midwest. I showed one of the storyboards of the TV commercials we were running in Italy and said it was our intent to eventually begin TV advertising in the US.

When we finished lunch, John Ferrara handed us a reorder. We were astonished at the size of the purchase.

In Chicago, our meeting with Sal Vinceguerra was equally successful. Once we introduced Brock, we allowed him to make the entire presentation regarding the billboard and TV programs. He took it upon himself to add his thoughts about using olive oil for frying, closing with the statement of how ridiculous it was for people to complain about the cost, and yet they buy cigarettes and inhale nicotine.

Sal laughed, reached in his pocket, and pulled out a package of cigarettes. "Well, Brock, I have been trying to quit, and you convinced me." He crumbled the package.

Laughing, we applauded him. The meeting ended on a high note. He, too, handed us a nice reorder.

Atlanta

The pilot of our plane circled over Atlanta as we approached the airport. As we got closer, some of the old antebellum plantation homes became visible. I recalled how General Sherman's hatred for the south made it easy to burn the city to the ground. Remarkably, in less than ninety years, it had become one of the most beautiful cities in the country. I was impressed.

We checked in to the Hotel Clermont located in the older section of the city. The weather was beautiful, and we decided to take a walk before dinner. Gina said, "I did not know of any great restaurants here, so we are dining at the hotel tonight."

At the restaurant, I asked the manager about their major purveyor. He replied, "Let me get their business card."

We asked the hotel concierge to make lunch and dinner reservations at Italian restaurants for the next day. At both restaurants, Brock got the important lesson about cold-calling. From those inquiries, we got two additional names of purveyors and met with all three the following day. The name of their distributor for Italian foods was unanimous; it was Salamone's Italian Foods. The owner's name was Pete Salamone. I called him and set up an appointment for the next morning.

Brock was quiet at the meeting. Pete Salamone was not initially interested in taking on distribution of another product. After Gina and I made our presentation, he said, "Thank you for your time, but my warehouse is bulging with products. In order to take on your oil, I would have to open another warehouse. It is cost prohibitive."

Brock, without any prompting, said, "Excuse me, Mr. Salamone. Before you reject our proposal, may I suggest you taste our oil. Aren't you interested in being on the ground floor of a new way to enjoy food? We have successful distributors in LA, St. Louis, Chicago, and Boston and all over Italy. If you like our oil, why not do a test and initially use public warehousing for shipping. If successful, then go to a larger warehouse. I will spend whatever time necessary to work with your purveyors to break the doors down to achieve success. For the record, we got your name from three others who tasted our oil and loved it."

Salamone looked at me and said, "Where did you find this guy? Let me taste the oil.

"Wow, this is the best olive oil I have ever tasted. Let's do this. I'll give you a *test* order with the provision that Brock returns when it arrives. I want him and one of my salesmen to work with the three purveyors you mentioned calling on some of their clients to see what happens. If they have success, I'll take you on."

I asked, "Excuse me, Pete. What states do you cover?"

"We call on purveyors—specialty-food stores only, no restaurants. Our business is primarily here in Atlanta, North and South Carolina, and Alabama. Most of our new business is done at trade shows. We depend on the purveyors to sell our canned tomatoes and cheeses."

I said, "Bravo! Write the order. We'll give you exclusivity in those states if we proceed to contract."

*****

Dallas

At dinner, Gina said, "Let's follow the same procedure in Dallas: get the names of the three best restaurants from the concierge when we check into the hotel then get the names of their purveyors and narrow it down to one or two distributors."

I agreed.

We arrived late in Dallas, and the restaurants were closed, including the one in our hotel. We had coffee and a piece of pie in the hotel café and called it a day. We got the names of several good Italian restaurants from the concierge before retiring.

At breakfast the next morning, we got a card bearing the name of the purveyor of the hotel restaurant.

Brock made all the presentations at the restaurants over the next two days, and we narrowed it down to two Italian food distributors: Toscana Italian Food Imports and Farnese Imports. Gina made the calls for appointments with both.

We met with Toscana in the morning. Brock made the presentation and did a great job. Mr. Toscana was very kind and complimented him and said, "Thank you, young man, and thank you, Gina and Giancarlo. I have to refuse your offer. We are a small firm with limited distribution, and there's no way we can do justice to your oil, so I have to say no."

Brock made one last attempt to pursue him, to no avail. I put my arm around him as we exited the office and said, "We'll get the next one, Brock. Don't be discouraged."

Our reception at Farnese Imports was entirely opposite the one at Toscana. I introduced Gina, Brock, and myself.

"My name is Frank Castellano. Thanks for being here."

Gina said, "Frank, where is your family from?"

"My mother and father were born in Sicily. My dad arrived in 1913, got a job mining coal in Alabama, and two years later, he sent for my mom."

Gina replied, "What part of Sicily? Giancarlo was born in Siracusa, and we have a home there."

"They emigrated from a small town called Ragusa."

I said, "That is crazy, Frank. Gina and I were there recently. We loved the city."

"I love it too. I am sure you people have more to do. tell me about your oil."

Brock wasted no time. He put the brochure on the table and did his routine. His confidence set the stage for him to speak with authority. The packaging presentation went just as smoothly. He climaxed by asking Frank to taste the oil.

Frank excused himself, left the room, and returned with his wife and a dish for the oil. "This is my wife, Josie. She heads up product development."

We exchanged greetings. They both tasted the oil and shook their heads with a positive grin on their faces. Frank looked at Josie and said, "What do you think, sweetheart?"

"I love it, Frank. My only concern is the price. In the past, when we thought about getting into the olive oil business, the margins were too low."

I put copies of the distributor price list in front of them and waited for their review. Frank was first to answer. He looked at Josie and said, "I think we are in the olive oil business, Jo. How soon can you get us in business, Giancarlo?"

"We can get you samples next week through our distributor in LA. We keep sample inventory there. Then perhaps in ten days to two weeks, Brock will return and begin training your sales people and calling on your clients. That brings up the next question. Frank. What states do you cover?"

"We cover Texas, Louisiana, and Tennessee."

"That's perfect. We have no distribution in those states."

"So, Giancarlo, did you bring a contract?"

Brock reached in his briefcase before Frank got the words out of his mouth and put the contract on the table. Frank and Josie both laughed. "Giancarlo, please leave this. Let me review it, and come back in the morning, and we will get it signed. If you don't mind, I'll write in the states we discussed."

I said, "If you need more time to review it with your attorney, Frank, we can come back the day after tomorrow."

"My lawyer is sitting next to me, Giancarlo, and she and I will review it. Thanks for your time. See you people in the morning. You are quite a team."

We met the next morning to sign the contract. I was surprised at the initial order Josie handed to me. It included a separate order for each of their warehouses in Dallas, New Orleans, and Memphis. Josie said, "There's a contingency with these purchase orders, Giancarlo. We want fifty cents a can and twenty-five cents a bottle for advertising money to promote your oil. Is it acceptable?"

"Not only is it acceptable, I'll go one better. Once we launch our billboard program in LA, we will run a six-month campaign in each of the three cities!"

Frank added one more request, "I want Brock to travel for two days with our sales reps in each city."

"I'll be there, Frank. I can't wait to see New Orleans."

Our goodbyes included warm hugs. It was the Italian way.

On the plane, I reached back to my early days as an enthusiastic young stockbroker. There was no fear. Buying stocks was like using Monopoly money, only it was real cash.

Brock Severino reminded me of myself. He had no fear. His confidence was his power.

I also thought about the cable I had sent to Salvatore regarding the field worker and his girlfriend. There was a cable at the house from Salvatore when we arrived. He initiated an investigation with the Lucca Police Department. Marco was assured that it was a routine investigation. The meeting was held at the office with the girlfriend in one room and Marco in another room. Both were asked similar questions, and the police determined none of our proprietary techniques had been exposed. There was an interesting disclosure—the girlfriend was originally from Bari, which is the heart of the olive oil production in Puglia. But she swore she was not connected to any oil-producing family. My mind once again referred to Emerson's rule: "What fears we have endured that failed to arrive."

I shared the news with Gina, and of course, she had to get the needle out. "See, aren't you glad I convinced you to send the cable? Now you can rest, knowing there's nothing to be concerned about."

I smiled and shook my head, avoiding handing her any satisfaction.

*****

February

Gina and I strolled into the country club dining room and headed to our favorite table. Out of nowhere, Sharon, Tony, Sandra, and Tom appeared and yelled, "Surprise!"

I had forgotten it was my birthday. After dinner, we moved to the bar, and Tom ordered a bottle of champagne, and they toasted me. Tony stood and said, "Giancarlo, you are a classic. You do not look anywhere near fifty-five years old. Keep doing what you're doing, and 'keep the old man out.' Bar him from the front door. We love you and are all grateful for the love and respect you have for us.!"

Tom excused himself to go to the washroom. As we walked out the front door, he was sitting in a beautiful 1955 Ford Thunderbird convertible with a red bow on it and a sign:

HAPPY BIRTHDAY HANDSOME

As tears rolled down the left side of my face, I grabbed Gina, gave her a warm embrace, and whispered, "Thanks. I love you."

The drive home in that car reminded me of the good fortune I have enjoyed my entire life—a great childhood; incredible, loving parents; and the innate ability to make money from a successful business career. Gina sat at the top of the list. The friends who took the time to celebrate my birthday stood out as another fortunate addition.

Gina's 1954 Corvette

Giancarlo's 1955 Thunderbird

CHAPTER 11

Lucca
April

The bright-red poppies were already vibrant on the Tuscan hills as we drove from Firenze to Lucca. Gina and I were delighted with the early bloom. I mentioned it to Salvatore, and he said, "Signora and Signore, it is due to the hot spring we have had, which means we will have an early harvest this year.

"Signore, when do you think we will begin our first trip to visit our distributors?"

"Salvatore, you and I are going into town tomorrow morning to buy your business shoes and clothes. While there, we will purchase a late-model Fiat for you. We'll be visiting our distributors in Milan and Verona. I'll let you know as soon as I make the appointments."

We were barely in the house when the aromas emanating from the kitchen ignited my appetite. Anna greeted us with that heart-warming smile that was always there. We were home.

Gina and I walked out to the patio and sat in the warm sunlight. A gentle breeze and the tall umbrella trees kept it comfortably cool. Gina was silent. It was always that way when something was bothering her. I knew the drill. Best I open the door and get it on the table before our food arrives. "So, my sweet, beautiful bride, what do I have to do to break the silent treatment?'

"Flattery works, handsome. Is there more?"

"There is—only after you explain the silence. We barely arrived, and you erect the cross, dig out your bag of nails and trusty hammer, and prepare to nail me to it."

"No, you have it all wrong, Hamlet. There's no plan for a cross. The imaginary wood is for the stage I was planning to erect. Please don't be so dramatic."

"I see, so please tell me what was causing the retraction of your sexy tongue."

"We just spent three nonstop months on the road, training and traveling with Brock. You have not relaxed, nor have I. And first thing before we even set foot in the house, you're planning on traveling with Salvatore. How about catching our breath and relaxing for a while. We will be here for three months. Why not plan the trips with nice breaks along the way so we can enjoy the reason we are here."

"Once again, my wise beauty queen, you get the prize for keeping me from venturing into the oversized doghouse. How do I ever thank you?"

"You better exercise by retracting that long tongue of yours and return this conversation the way it began—with silence."

We both laughed.

The next morning, we went to town with Salvatore. Gina took charge and began helping him with his wardrobe selections. My mind drifted back to 1922, when I started at the brokerage house. Tom Venegoni took me to a haberdashery on Fifth Avenue and helped me with my clothing and shoe purchases. The wardrobe purchase was only part of it. The education lessons and advice from Tom and his guidance were like earning a degree from Harvard's business school. It was my turn to give back.

When Gina and Salvatore were finished, Salvatore attempted to pay for the clothing and shoes. Gina stopped him. "This is our treat, Salvatore."

"No, signora. I have been saving my pay for this day."

I stepped in. "Salvatore, please learn in dealing with my wife. She is the *boss*, understand?"

He looked at her and graciously accepted our generosity.

We went to the Fiat dealer and bought a 1953 four-door sedan. It was like new. Salvatore drove it back to the villa. He was like a kid with a new electric train set.

I followed Gina's wishes and held back on traveling. The news on TV was mixed. Segregation and the Civil Rights Movement were always prevalent. Congress passed the Protection of Civil Rights Act, making it a federal offense to practice evil things against African Americans. There were demonstrations all through the South. Organized black groups would sit at counters in restaurants until they were served, and if service was refused, they would sit there, tying up the seats. This issue was not going away anytime soon.

The other news was the introduction of new inventions. Zenith had invented a gadget to automatically change channels by remote control. Another new invention was the microwave oven for cooking. TV was boosting the economy by promoting them, and the advertising commercials dominated prime time.

The economy in the US was booming, led by the automobile business. Detroit's designers were on a roll beginning in 1955 with extreme changes in their designs. Chevrolet dramatically changed the style of the 1955 Bel Air. An automatic transmission and a V8 cylinder engine were options. Ford introduced the Thunderbird sports car to compete with Chevrolet's Corvette, and the battle for innovative automobile supremacy was on.

A campaign to buy American goods was started by the major manufacturers. It was designed to offset inexpensive Japanese products and those arriving from Germany. Brand names dominated TV commercials that pushed the theme "buy American made products to help the American economy." It was featured on all three networks.

Gina and I discussed some of the inventions that were making life easier and allowing people to enjoy life. The first GPS was launched, and the cordless phone was introduced, although very expensive.

Innovative things such as the heart pacemaker and bypass surgery were established. And women flocked to doctors' offices for the first birth control pill. This would have a huge impact on their lives, planning family growth and allowing them to contemplate working outside of the home.

Rock and roll continued to dominate the music business. A sexy, good-looking kid by the name of Elvis Presley made his debut on TV in Shreveport, Louisiana, and it went viral across the country. Black entertainers continued to dominate the music world. Technology was driving the US economy's rapid growth, and the women's movement and desegregation were changing the cultural landscape.

*****

Gina, always knowing the right time for everything, joined me one morning on the patio, kissed the top of my head, and said, "Well, handsome, are you ready to hit the road with Salvatore?"

"Only if you choose to join us. I can't bear the thought of being away from you."

"Are you looking for something special with that line?"

"No, but come to think of it, perhaps you might want to serve me with a kiss somewhere besides the top of my head."

Ignoring the quip, Gina asked, "Where are you thinking of starting with Salvatore? I am planning on joining you. I also want to plan a trip here in Tuscany."

"I want to start in Milan. It has been awhile since our last trip. I want to spend an hour or so with you and Salvatore going over the presentation so he has an idea of what to expect. That would give him time for questions."

Gina nodded in agreement.

Later that night, we saw the movie *The Rose Tattoo* with Anna Magnani, another Italian actress. It costarred Burt Lancaster and was adapted from Tennessee Williams's Broadway play. Filmed in Key West, Florida, Anna plays the part of a widow. She falls into deep depression after the death of her husband and becomes a recluse. Later, she learns of the former husband's infidelity, and it helps cure her depression.

Along comes a lodger (her costar, Burt Lancaster), a truck driver who rents a room in her building. A romance commences, and they fall in love. She becomes pregnant with his child, and they marry.

As we walked out of the theater, I commented to Gina, "In the past, the Legion of Decency would have prevented distribution of that movie." Thanks to the persistence of the stalwarts of the movie industry, they defeated the Legion of Decency, and it no longer exists. Open minds and adult approach have won over the past scrutiny of the legion.

Gina replied, "Thank goodness the Legion of Decency no longer has that control over the creative mind and thought."

The next morning, we went for coffee and the newspaper. For a change, there was some good news. A vaccine for polio, the crippling disorder, was introduced by scientist Jonas Salk. It immediately was approved by the Food and Drug Administration. This alleviated the fear that had permeated the lives of new parents. They could breathe with a sigh of relief.

After breakfast, we stopped at the record store. There was a major table displaying copies of Frank Sinatra's latest hit. We bought a copy of "In the Wee Small Hours of the Morning," which was a major comeback after winning the Academy Award as supporting actor in *From Here to Eternity*. Old blue eyes was not out to pasture yet.

*****

May

We drove to Milan for our meeting with our distributor Don Giovani Ruggeri. It was a hot, balmy day. I made a mental note—my next car would have air-conditioning. The heat was somewhat offset by the never-ending scenery driving through Tuscany and later by the charming, beautiful, historic towns and villages of Lombardy. Driving through the hills of Tuscany on the way to Milan is a journey filled with breathtaking scenery and timeless charm. As you wind through the rolling hills, you pass vineyards and olive groves—the neatly arranged rows stretching out like a patchwork quilt. Medieval hilltop villages dot the landscape, their ancient stone buildings and red-tiled roofs standing proudly against the backdrop of lush green countryside.

Don Giovani greeted Gina and me with a hug, and warmly extended his hand to Salvatore. They had spoken on the phone, but this was their first meeting in person. Gina presented the boards displaying the commercials we planned to run in the fall. Don Giovani smiled and said, "I guess you're looking for a large reorder next?"

Gina jokingly said, "Signore, let's just say we will not refuse it if you're offering one."

I added, "Don Giovanni, Salvatore has a new role. He will want to begin working with your purveyors and your salesmen, calling on existing customers and new ones to introduce our advertising campaign. He will be stressing the healthy aspects of cooking with our oil and the unhealthy use of lard."

"I like the idea, Giancarlo. How long will you be in Milan?"

"We will be leaving in the morning, signore."

"Well, then let's have dinner tonight, and I'll bring you a nice reorder for both bottles and cans. Do you mind if we dine at Antica Trattoria della Pesa tonight?"

Gina said, "Signore, it's our favorite restaurant in Milan."

Later that evening, Don Giovani introduced us to his wife, Sophia. The manager greeted Don Giovani with a hug in the traditional Italian custom. It was obvious they were longtime friends. He warmly greeted Gina and me, and I introduced Salvatore.

Once seated, Don Giovani handed me the wine list, and while I was reviewing it, our waiter approached the table with warm bread and the traditional baby veal meatballs. I heard a loud "Oh my god" from Gina. I looked up as he poured oil on a plate from a bottle of our oil.

The manager approached our table and asked if we had tasted the meatballs. He looked at Don Giovani, and they exchanged sly grins. Don Giovani could no longer contain himself and said, "The second surprise is the meatballs. After sixty years frying their meatballs in lard, they are now fried in Lucca olive oil."

Gina smiled broadly. I could not believe what had just happened. I complimented the manager and thanked Don Giovani for his effort to convince his friend to change their history-old tradition. It was quite an experience for Salvatore.

The next day, the weather had cooled, and our drive to Lucca was more pleasant than the previous day. We stopped in Alba for lunch, and Salvatore expressed how grateful he was for the experience. He apologized for remaining quiet throughout the previous day.

Once back at the villa, Gina and I discussed Salvatore's silence during the activities. She said, "Salvatore is a nice man, but I am concerned about his lack of participation. Perhaps I am making a comparison to Brock and Evan."

"Let's not rush to judgment, Gina. Let me spend time with him. For now, I want to relax, spend some time reading, eating some good food, listening to our music, and watching TV."

"Well, that's a switch. I thought for sure that with the success we just had, you'd be ready to hit the road again, I like the new you."

June

I walked out to the patio and was met by a beautiful sunrise. The sun had the sky to itself, not a cloud to obscure its brilliance. The heat had already burned off the dew on the grass. It was one of those days to spend outside, a gentle breeze completed the splendor.

Soon, I received my early-morning affection as Gina stood over me and kissed the top of my head. "Good morning, Giancarlo. Did you sleep well?"

"I did. Thanks, Gina. I know you did. You did not snore."

"Hmm, I assume there's a compliment coming. You certainly want to avoid being in a small shelter normally used to keep puppies from the cold and rain."

"You know how much I love your charming personality early in the morning, don't you?

"I have invited Salvatore to join us for breakfast to discuss our next trip. I want him to feel part of it."

"I think it's a good idea, Giancarlo. Let's have him make the early presentation of the brochure and packaging. I'll do the TV storyboards, and you can explain his new role."

I heard Salvatore walking up the steps from our downstairs entry. Gina saw him first and exclaimed, "Bravo, Salvatore, you look like you just stepped out of *Esquire* magazine!"

He was dressed in his new shoes, slacks, and blue blazer. And before he could comment, Anna approached with a large platter of her croissants and a wonderful egg frittata. She took one look at Salvatore, smiled, and said, "Excuse me, Salvatore, are you going to mass? Today is Tuesday. You look so nice."

Salvatore modestly smiled, but he was at a loss for words. All he could do was smile and say, "Grazie."

I said, "That's enough, ladies. Let's be careful. We don't want Salvatore to get any ideas about heading to Milan to be a model."

Everyone laughed.

We sat down for breakfast. As usual Salvatore was quiet. The silence was short-lived once we finished breakfast and the table was cleared. "Signora and Giancarlo, before we begin discussing our next trip, I'd like to discuss the business here in Tuscany. As you know, we deal primarily with purveyors. We have never had a distributor. The business is satisfactory but has not grown much in the last ten years. We get phone reorders and some in the mail. No one has called on these purveyors in years.

"We have been using inventory of our old packaging on their orders. I was impressed with everything you presented at our recent meeting. I'd like your permission to begin calling on our customers in the area. I know all of them from phone conversations but have never met them. I am confident I can make the presentations. I took the liberty to make an appointment this afternoon with the purveyor in town. Please show me the courtesy to keep the date with her."

Gina was beaming. His statement added to what had already been a good day. "Salvatore, you would not be sitting here if we didn't believe in your ability to succeed. We are overwhelmed with what you just said. By all means, keep that appointment. What other cities are you planning to visit?"

"I had a feeling you might want to discuss this. I want to see existing clients in Pisa, San Remo, Siena, and Livorno. But we do not have anyone in Volterra or Grosseto, and I'd like to call on both cities. More importantly, we should plan on spending some time in Firenze. We have a good client there, but again, no one has spent any time with him."

Gina said, "Salvatore, I love this idea. Bring samples of every-thing with you to leave with the purveyors. Maybe plan an hour with their salesmen in the presentations."

"Signora I am planning on doing that. Giancarlo, are you and la Signora aware that our purveyor in town is a woman? Her name is Maria Antinora. She is the owner of Antinora Food and Cheese. Her husband started the business in 1932. During the war, he was killed when the city was bombed by the Allies. They had three young boys, and the business died with her husband.

"Her parents lived in a small villa not far from here, and after the war, they sold the villa, and Maria resurrected the business with the money. She is a strong woman. The entire family works in the business, including her grandmother and grandfather."

"Wow, Salvatore, I am embarrassed. I have taken our business here for granted. Giuseppe Fragale never discussed it with me."

"Don't feel badly, Giancarlo. She doesn't show any emotion about what happened. I had to drag the story out of her."

Gina said, "Salvatore, next time you make an appointment with her, we will join you. We want to meet her."

We thanked Salvatore, wished him good luck, and after he left, I looked at Gina and said, "I am more confident than ever we made the right decision in promoting him."

Gina added, "Firenze is our next trip, Giancarlo. Why didn't we think of what he just said to us?"

*****

Salvatore called me two days after the enlightening breakfast we shared and asked for a brief meeting. He was beaming when he walked into my study. I knew he had good news to share. "So, Signore Vitale, I presume you have a success story from your meeting."

With a smile ear to ear, he showed me the order he received. It was incredible. He was as proud as a peacock. "Giancarlo, this is not an ordinary purveyor. I had a tour of their office and warehouse. They distribute pasta, Parmigiano and Asiago cheese, salami and prosciutto, wine from Tuscany, canned tomatoes from San Marzano, and of course, our oil. Signora Antinora wants to meet you and Gina and asked if it's possible to become the exclusive distributor for Lucca Olive Oil in Tuscany!"

"Wow, Salvatore, that's hard to believe. We have been asleep. Let's let that be our next trip. We are free next week. Please set up a meeting. We want to meet her."

We met the following week in their office dining room. Just about every pastry known to Italians was on the table. We were greeted like family. The grandmother and grandfather were dressed in their Sunday best, as were the three sons. Salvatore introduced us. Maria Antinora shook our hands with a strong grip. She was movie-star beautiful and was dressed like she just walked off the runway at a Milan fashion show.

We briefly talked about Gina's background and mine. I explained Salvatore told us about the story of what happened in World War II.

We toured the office. Six women were busy at their typewriters. Next was the enormous warehouse. There was a walk-in cooler where the cheese and meat products were stored and a large thermostatically controlled area for pasta storage. It was more impressive than any distributor's facility we had visited.

We returned to the office, and my first question was, "Maria, do you service Firenze?"

"Giancarlo, we service all of Tuscany, all the top purveyors. We do not know of any other firm that stocks the inventory we have. If I may be so bold, unless you are prepared to give us exclusive distribution rights for all of Tuscany, we are not interested in entering into a contract. Allow me to explain why I insist. We guarantee overnight delivery when we receive an order for any product. To achieve that requires carrying serious inventory. We have sixty purveyors and another seventy-two grocery stores we cater to."

"Signora, I made up my mind to offer you an exclusive contract when I met you and your family an hour ago. I have a contract in my briefcase for you to review with your attorney."

"Giancarlo, I don't spend money with lawyers. May I see the contract? No matter what it says, the deal is between me and you. It only works if we are both good businesspeople. We have been doing business with your company since my husband started the business in the '30s."

We signed the contract and parted with hugs. When we got to the car, I put my arm around Salvatore and congratulated him. We went to our favorite restaurant Buca di Sant'Antonio for lunch.

*****

Siracusa
July

Vincenzo picked us up in Catania at noon. He told us that Alena wasn't feeling well and had not stocked the kitchen. We decided to have lunch at a restaurant. It was unusually hot. Fortunately, the restaurant had a shady area under a group of trees that provided relief from the sun. When we arrived, Gina insisted Alena should rest.

After lunch, Gina went to the market and shopped for groceries. Unbeknownst to me, she stopped in the travel agent's office. We spent the rest of the afternoon relaxing and reading at the villa.

With Alena resting, we elected to eat dinner at our favorite trattoria that evening. After we ordered, I said, "Gina, the representative from the travel agent's office called and left some alternate days for the secret cruise you planned."

Dead silence, and a stare with a *fungha* (an old Sicilian dialect, the word for mushroom) appeared on Gina's face. I made a comment about the heat. Gina continued the stare and finally smiled. "We will discuss the secret trip when we get home, wise owl. Meanwhile, you have ample time to decide your penance. Will it be the puppy house or use of your shovel?"

Alena returned to the kitchen the next day, and our food fest returned with her. I put candles on the table and had two glasses of wine ready. I asked Gina to sit while I served the food. She looked at me, smiling. "I'm amazed at how distressed you get when the threat of digging and your favorite retreat is presented."

"So, my love, I can't wait to hear about the cruise."

"Let's eat, and if I decide to move forward with it, I'll share it with you."

I continued the verbal tennis match through dinner, and we finally got serious. "Giancarlo, we just concluded a stressful six months of business, and I want to take a cruise to Capri. We have been all over Sicily and Italy and never visited that wonderful historical city. Is it all right with you?"

"Absolutely! Does my acceptance get me a reprieve from the suffering I have been going through the past six hours?"

"Yes, as long as you go to the refrigerator and get the cannolis."

Over the next few days, I decided to forgo the news both in the newspaper and on TV until it was time to leave for the Capri cruise. Vincenzo drove us to Catania, and we boarded the cruise ship to Capri. The Tyrrhenian Sea was like glass, and the weather was glorious. A gentle sea breeze kept the sun's heat bearable.

We checked in to Hotel Quisisana in time for dinner. Later, we walked the area around the hotel. It seemed like everyone strolling the area was in a best-dressed contest. This was not the slums of Manhattan. We learned from a brochure in the room that the city dated back to the early Roman days and was a favorite of Caesar Augustus dating to 29 BC.

After breakfast the next morning, we walked the entire city. Gina spent a lot of time in the fancy shops but remained her conservative self and didn't make a purchase. We took a small shuttle bus to Anacapri high above the city, a quaint retreat away from the tourists. We had lunch reservations at Da Paolino and sat under the shade branches of a monster lemon tree. The scent of the lemons was overshadowed by the fresh-bread smells from the kitchen.

Lunch was beyond description—chicken breast served with a lemon-reduced cream sauce that endured our bread dipping. It was the best meal of the three days.

The trip to Capri highlighted our stay in Siracusa. The rest of the six weeks was spent reading and seeing movies, notably, *East of Eden* with Jo Van Fleet and James Dean. The movie was based on John Steinbeck's novel. Dean was constantly seeking the approval of his religious father. The father always made comparisons favorable to the rival brother. Steinbeck compared the brothers to biblical Cain and Abel. The difficult relationship between Dean and his father was never resolved due to a stroke suffered by the father.

There was severe criticism of the book and movie by the critics due to the language, stereotyping various ethnicities, child molestation, and the brothel frequented by the Dean character. Those elements did not make for a happy ending. We did not like the movie because it was depressing.

*****

Los Angeles
November

Evan and Brock picked us up and drove us to a lunch meeting with Sam Marzullo, our distributor. We drove down Century Boulevard to La Cienega and were surprised to see our billboard. It stunned us. Sam praised the boys for their efforts with the purveyors and restaurants. The discussion regarding the importance of advertising was the main topic. Sam wanted TV as the next stage, and we agreed. I promised him I would get with our agency and come up with a co-op program for him and the purveyors.

Palm Springs
December

I placed a call to Brock and asked him to move back to the Midwest. I gave him his choice: St. Louis or Chicago. His territory was the entire Midwest, but he'd have to cover Atlanta and Boston until I could hire and train someone for the East Coast. He elected St. Louis, stating he could live at home until the need for an apartment became necessary.

"Brock, I want you to break off all ties to California and be in St. Louis the first of the year."

He agreed and wished me happy holidays. "Please give my best regards to Gina."

114

The group of us, including the Marzullos, brought in 1956 with a quiet evening at our house. Gina, Sandra, and Sharon cooked a gourmet dinner, and Sam brought everyone's favorite wine. I couldn't think of a better way to welcome the new year.

Giuseppe Vitale

Located at the corner of LaCienega and Century boulevard

CHAPTER 12

Palm Springs
January 1956

I woke up with one thing on my mind: Lucca and some changes I wanted to make. I cabled Salvatore to have him include his brother Giuseppe on some of his calls to clients in Tuscany. I also requested he find a suitable assistant for Giuseppe because ultimately, I would have him move to Bologna to service our distributors in the east. With that taken care of, I looked forward to the day with Tony and Sharon.

At breakfast, Sharon suggested we go to a matinee and see the movie *Lust for Life* about the Dutch artist Vincent van Gogh. The movie was based on van Gogh's abusive life and his struggles. It featured Kirk Douglas as van Gogh and Anthony Quinn as his friend, artist Paul Gauguin. Sharon said both Douglas and Quinn were nominated for Academy Awards. After seeing the movie, we agreed it was well portrayed by both actors, but Anthony Quinn was outstanding, and he dominated the movie.

Van Gogh left Holland for Paris, seeking inspiration, and became friends with Gauguin. They drank excessive amounts of Pernod, an anise-based alcoholic liqueur. The original blend was an absinthe, and it was thought to have psychoactive effects. Some thought it had to do with van Gogh's severe mental problems. Van Gogh's paintings were not understood by the average art lover. Many were a reflection of his struggles to find inspiration and get through his day-to-day life.

His mental health issues, which included hallucinations and delusions, were not common knowledge. By age thirty-three, his mental illness put him in and out of mental asylums. He was not eating, subsisting on bread, coffee, and cigarettes.

Another unknown fact is that most of his eight hundred oil canvases and two thousand sketches were done in the last few years of his life. His mental illness led to many rumors about him, such as cutting off his ear (it was the lobe, not the entire ear) and his presumed death by suicide, which actually may have been murder based on the evidence. Now, years later, mental illness is still not well understood or treated.

Back at home, it was another day of work. I placed calls to Evan and Brock, and they updated me on recent activities. I told Brock it was time to hire a person to handle the East Coast as liaison with our distributors in Boston and Atlanta. That person would intern with him for ninety days before taking on the responsibility.

I called Ricardo Pozzini next and asked him to search for someone for us to interview, and he promised he'd find someone. I made a similar call to Pete Salamone in Atlanta about a replacement for Brock. Pete asked, "Does it have to be a man?"

I replied, "I do not have a problem hiring a woman as long as she is willing to travel the New England area and the states you cover."

Pete was quick to suggest a young woman, Nancy Garrett, who had been interning with him for seven summers while in high school and college. She was to graduate in May. Pete explained, "Giancarlo, she knows the food business. She's bright and makes a nice appearance and has the personality for sales. She handles our phone order desk and processes all mail orders. She also works part-time while attending classes."

"Pete, she sounds perfect. Talk to her about the job and have her call me if she's interested. By the way, how's your business?"

Laughing, he said, "Giancarlo, do you see our reorders? Our business is great. Brock is an amazing kid. I will hate to lose him."

"Well, it will be a while before you lose him. His replacement will spend ninety days in Lucca then another ninety days training with Brock, so you have half a year with him. Thanks for your time, Pete."

With my work done, Gina and I went to the bookstore. We bought *Andersonville* by MacKinlay Kantor and *The Last Hurrah* by Edwin O'Connor. I was shocked to see a table featuring *Playboy* magazine. I thumbed through it, but the "boss" soon showed up and snatched it from my hand and put it back on the table. "You're a dirty old man, Giancarlo. Don't be getting any ideas."

Smiling, I said, "What are you, a recent hire for the Legion of Decency? I was reading a story. Besides, the cover had a nice photo of Marilyn Monroe."

"Yes, and you were mesmerized by her nude body."

Our next stop was the record store. We needed some new music. There was a table display of Fats Domino's latest hit "Blueberry Hill," another with a life-size poster of Elvis Presley and his big hits "Don't Be Cruel" and "Blue Suede Shoes," and a similar tribute to Ella Fitzgerald's "The Lady Is a Tramp." We bought all three albums. We were eager to get more acquainted with Presley's music.

The Vietnam War continued to dominate the TV news. It became known as "the Television War." The coverage was uncensored, having a significant effect on the American people, concerned that their children could ultimately be drafted into the war. Public opinion began to turn against the war. It was believed the American people were being fed lies. TV showed South Vietnam military abuse against the Vietnamese people, which increased protest. Demand to end US participation began to flood the news. Dissension among the leaders of South Vietnam surfaced, and this chess game was featured on the news and continued to be disturbing.

*****

Salvatore responded to my cable and was happy to promote Giuseppe and suggested we promote longtime Sicilian employee Andreino Puglisi as assistant. He needed a few weeks to train Andreino before having Giuseppe join him on the road. I responded with my approval and told him to proceed.

The sun finally returned from its weeklong sabbatical, and Tony and I resumed our golf game.

February

With my upcoming birthday, I wanted to get away to celebrate. Gina suggested we drive to Carmel-by-the-Sea and made hotel reservations at the Lodge at Pebble Beach. We departed the day before my birthday and took the scenic road along the Pacific Ocean. The sun followed us, giving the drive added pleasure.

After the eight-hour drive, we checked in to the lodge, the golf course hotel. It is situated along the scenic course with a splendid view of the Pacific Ocean. It was dinnertime, and we were both famished. We dropped our bags in the room and immediately departed for the dining room. We stopped dead in our tracks at the entrance of the dining room and were stunned! Our friends Judy and Jimmy Boscamp were sitting at a table just inside the door. They were as shocked as we were. They both jumped up to hug us.

We had not seen them since my birthday celebration in Antibe in 1950. We joined them, and we began catching up on the past five years. Jimmy was first: "So, Giancarlo, how is the retirement going? Are you getting bored?"

Gina was quick to answer, "The retirement lasted a year, Jimmy. We are in the olive-oil business. Giancarlo has taken over marketing his family's business. You didn't really think he could retire and grow old gracefully, did you?"

"I don't know why I asked, Gina."

Judy asked, "Jimmy, tell them about your latest move."

"We just relocated to Beverly Hills. I am executive vice president for Bank of America's loan department for Southern California. I oversee all commercial, industrial, and home loans from San Diego to San Jose."

"Congratulations, Jimmy! That's a long way from Chicago, where you started working with me."

"Giancarlo, I will never forget what you did for me. I was a green kid when you took me under your wing, and taught me the banking business. I owe everything I have achieved to your trust and confidence."

"Nonsense, Jimmy. You worked your butt off and deserve to be where you are. Let's have some dinner. We are starving, and dinner is on us."

"That is not happening, Giancarlo. You always get the check. This is my tab."

Jimmy and I played the golf course the next two days while the ladies had lunch and shopped. We dined together both nights and said our goodbyes the next morning and agreed to get together later in the month. As we parted, we extended them an invitation to stay with us in Palm Springs.

I received the call from Nancy Garrett when we returned and liked her spirit. She spoke with confidence and left no doubt in my mind she could be the first female salesperson for our company. She agreed to fly to LA to meet us immediately for the formal interview. She stated she had her résumés in the hands of several firms and wanted to secure a position before she graduated.

I admired her aggressive approach and told her I'd have our travel agent send her a plane ticket. We agreed to meet the following weekend.

I began reading *Andersonville*, which is about the Confederate prisoner of war camp in the South. The estimate was that forty-five to fifty thousand union soldiers were confined there. Over fourteen thousand died in the short time between 1864 and 1865 when the civil war ended.

There is no accounting of those who survived and were released with diseases contracted while confined. Most died from scurvy, dysentery, and starvation. The original design of the facility was to house twenty thousand people. Living conditions were horrendous. The command of the prison was under the direction of a man named Ransom Chadwick, who was tried for war crimes after the war ended and was executed.

This book enlightened the American people of the horrors of war inflicted on its own people. People in general had allowed time since the end of the war to fade away. Few realized that more than six hundred thousand Americans died in it. The exact count of those who returned with missing body parts and permanent disabilities is unknown. I thought about our soldiers who were returning home with life-changing injuries from the current war. When would the insanity end?

Brock called me the next morning with disturbing news. "Giancarlo, I was in a discount grocery store just checking on some cheap olive oil that was advertised. It is in a nondescriptive bottle. The oil is pale yellow as opposed to our deep green color. I bought a small can and bottle, and I'm sending them to you."

"Thanks, Brock. Check out the extent of these cheap olive oils in grocery stores. How widespread is the distribution? Also, get me the prices and any other information about its origins."

"Will do. I am enclosing the receipt in the package."

March

When we met with Nancy Garrett, I was pleased to see she was dressed well, and her answers to our questions regarding her goals in life were astounding. She left no doubt her experience working for Pete and her education prepared her for any profession. She presented her résumé the minute we sat down to lunch. It, too, was impressive.

I had already made the decision to hire her, so I was not prepared for her questions. She spoke with confidence. "Mrs. and Mr. Giambrone, I have a few questions. First, what is the starting salary for the position we are discussing? What are the job responsibilities? Where will I be required to live? Does your company have a retirement program? Do you provide medical insurance? Will I be required to travel, and if so, do you pay travel expenses? Do you pay initial clothing compensation?"

Gina smiled and said, "I will yield to Mr. Giambrone to answer those questions."

"Nancy, your questions are excellent." I answered about the job responsibilities and told her she could live either in Atlanta or Boston. I explained we did not have a retirement program, but I stated it is something we would be thinking about and that I'd get back to her on it.

I said the health-insurance question was another one to review. The pay was a fifty-dollar-a-week salary plus commission incentives based on existing volume. The incentive would begin with the growth from that statistic. Travel expenses would be compensated, and yes, we would provide an initial clothing allowance.

Nancy had no further questions. We finished lunch with no final decision and agreed to talk later in the week. We returned to the airport for her flight back to Atlanta. The minute we dropped her off, Gina said, "Hire her, Giancarlo. I predict she will be your leader in the states. She is a diamond."

"I have already made the decision. I hope she agrees to join us."

Later that week, the cheap olive oil samples from Brock arrived. I was shocked. They were labeled olive oil. I showed them to Gina, and she suggested we take them to the US Food and Drug Administration in LA. The people who are labeling this are misleading the public. Something needed to be done about it.

I delayed our flight to Italy for a few days and made the call per Gina's suggestion. We visited with the Food and Drug Administration the following week, and after they saw the fake oil, they acknowledged this was common in all products and that they were handicapped. There was nothing they could do about it. The agent said, "It's the age-old warning, 'Let the buyer beware.'"

I took the samples back and decided to take them to Italy for a meeting with the economic development department. Italy needed to get involved because the label on both packaging said, "Made in Italy!"

A few days later, Nancy Garrett called and said, "Mr. Giambrone, I am happy to inform you, if you'll have me, I would love to join your firm."

"Welcome aboard, Nancy. We are elated. Here's the plan: after you graduate, my travel agent will send you a ticket to Italy. You'll fly to Rome, and one of our people will pick you up and drive you to Lucca, where you'll train throughout the harvest and pressing of the olives. Then you'll spend ninety days calling on clients with Brock, and then we will move you to a permanent position. Have you decided where you want to live?"

"I have, Mr. Giambrone. I want to live in Atlanta. For the record, I know most of Pete's clients."

"That will help. Congratulations, Nancy. We are happy to have you. Please give my regards to Pete." I hung up elated about our new hire.

CHAPTER 13

Lucca
April

Our flight from New York to Rome encountered horrendous turbulence due to strong winds. The stewardesses were prohibited from serving food. Our arrival was two hours late, and we barely made our connection to Firenze. We were starving by the time we arrived in Lucca.

Anna had dinner ready when we walked in. We were like two prisoners eating with both hands. Gina looked at me and began laughing, "Look at us. Slow down, Giancarlo. No one's going to come and take your food away."

"Excuse me, signora, but I was watching you a few minutes ago. You have marinara sauce on your blouse and sleeve and all over your lips, *sugo* mouth."

"What is *sugo*?"

"It's an old Sicilian dialect word for tomato sauce."

We both laughed.

Jet lag caught up with me, and I was up as the sun rose the next morning. Gina heard me rise and rolled over and fell asleep.

Anna was in the kitchen making bread. She was surprised when I strolled in for coffee. We exchanged good mornings, and she said the first loaves of bread would be out of the oven in a few minutes, and she'd bring me toast, butter, and jam.

The spring heat had already arrived when I walked out on the patio. Fortunately, a gentle breeze tamed it. I tempered my anxiety about visiting the Department of Commerce and Economic

Development regarding the cheap imitation oil Brock had sent me, knowing there'd be objections from Gina.

She joined me as Anna approached with a platter of toast. "You were up bright and early, Mr. Giambrone. I'm sure getting to Milan with the fake olive oil is why you couldn't sleep."

"Wrong, Mrs. Sigmund Freud. It was jet lag. I don't need early-morning analysis, and good morning to you."

Laughing, she came over and kissed my forehead, "Let's start over. Good morning, love of my life."

"That's much better. Do you want to go to Milan with me?"

"Sure. Can I have a cup of coffee first?"

After breakfast, I met with Salvatore and Giuseppe and reviewed sales for the first three months of the year. The numbers were outstanding, and further study showed the large reorders were coming from the regions where we had initiated TV advertising. It prompted me to expand the program to all our areas of distribution, including Tuscany.

We also looked at the inventory in the warehouse. Salvatore said we have enough to get through the rest of the season based on current sales. We studied last year's yield and decided unless there was major growth in volume, we would have enough oil to get us through 1957.

We concluded the meeting. Salvatore said Andreino was ready to assume the day-to-day activities, and he and Giuseppe would be on the road the following two weeks, calling on purveyors.

As we parted, he said, "Giancarlo, we are getting a few complaints from the distributors in Verona and Bologna. It is taking eight to ten days to receive their reorders. You might want to have a discussion with Alimondo, our trucking company." I added that to the to-do list.

I put off the trip to Milan for a couple of days to relax and read, knowing Gina would prefer it. I began reading *The Last Hurrah*, which is about an old-time Democratic mayor in Boston. He was the typical Irish leader, running for reelection and raising campaign money for his friend running for governor. His name was Frank Skeffington, and his friend was James Michael, also Irish.

His Republican opponent was a World War II hero with no political experience and no connections to the political machine. He chose to use the power of TV appearances and advertising. He and his fellow Republican running for governor defeated both of the Irishmen.

Irish Democrats controlled politics for over a century. They had power and money stemming from providing government jobs, as well as donations from businessmen and corporations, all key to maintaining control. Graft was an additional source of income.

The Democrat machine made large campaign contributions to incumbents at all levels of government—local, state, and federal. In many elections, the incumbents ran with no opposition. Such was politics in Boston and beyond.

We went to town for a cappuccino, and as we passed the appliance store, a colored TV set was displayed in the window. We went in to look and impulsively bought it. It cost $1,000.

Gina was aghast. "Giancarlo, you are forbidden to go to town for the rest of our stay. I can't believe what you just did."

I pulled out a dollar bill and waved it in front of her. "Gina, there's only two things you can do with this: sit and look at it all day or spend it. I have worked my butt off my entire life. Once in a while, if I find something that allows us to enjoy life a little more, I intend on splurging. We are only in this world for a *hot* minute. We are not going to deny ourselves anything."

Back at home, I turned to the news of the presidential election, which was heating up. Adlai Stevenson won the Democratic nomination, and President Eisenhower opted to run against him again. The polls were favoring the president, being a war hero. He had a clean personal life, no harmful baggage. Everything was in his favor—a strong economy, virtually no unemployment, peace, low taxes, and a happy constituency.

Stevenson, on the other hand, was seen as an old-school politician. Republicans told the media that he had debts to pay to the politicians who nominated him. Favors were expected from big businesses that provided large donations to his campaign

May

My mind was sharp as Gina and I drove to Milan for our first appointment with the economic development department. The representatives were astounded at the cheap oil. They assured me they would find the maker and take serious action to stop the fake labeling of the olive oil containers. Also, the lab chemists would be searching the contents to determine the oil used. I stressed they should establish strict laws regarding content labeling. It needed to be similar to the labeling for wine.

We next paid a visit to the Accardi Soap Company we had visited on our last trip. We were assured that the use of olive oil was a work in progress and that we'd be hearing from them in the next twelve months.

Our next stop was at La vie en Rose cosmetics. We were warmly greeted, and they, too, assured us they would soon have product for our review using our oil.

At our final meeting, Alimondo Trucking, I put our distributor locations for all of Italy on the table. While Bologna and Verona were the key issues, I stressed we needed a plan for the entire country. "Service is the only thing you have to sell. As a customer, we have been loyal from the day you started your business. Your business is no different than our business. The distributors we have in Verona and Bologna can replace us with oil from Puglia tomorrow morning."

"We hear you, Signore Giambrone. Please give us a few days to study the problem. I will need time to come up with a solution."

"Signore, I want a plan that guarantees three-day delivery from Lucca to anywhere in Italy. If it requires a slight upcharge for certain areas, we are willing to absorb it."

We agreed on the plan, and the meeting ended on a high note.

When we returned, a cable from Evan was waiting for us.

> Giancarlo I hate to be the bearer of bad
> news. We are seeing Spanish olive oil appearing
> in all the major grocery stores. It's appearing in

the chains like Ralph's. I have discussed this with
Brock and Nancy and they are witnessing it too.

I cabled back and asked him to buy a few samples and send them to Salvatore so we could test the contents and to include the prices. Gina asked, "What can you do, Giancarlo? This will have a serious effect on the business in the future."

"Gina, competition never hurts unless you allow it to penetrate your clients. We have a better product. We have a head start on the Spanish producers. We must stress our quality and get our distributors on board to promote our strengths. But first, we need to know what we are dealing with. How good or bad is their oil? We need to carefully monitor our sales. Let's not panic. We have good distribution and an excellent customer base."

Siracusa
July

The warm sea breezes somewhat reduced the July heat, and the salt air was a welcome feeling on the drive to Villa Giambrone. We momentarily left Lucca and the problems of the past six months. Alena had our favorite meal on the table within minutes of our arrival. I asked Gina if she wanted a glass of vino, and she replied with a definite yes.

"Giancarlo, can we have a few days for us. Please put the olive-oil business in the closet for a while."

"What olive oil business? I have no idea what you're talking about, lady."

Both the lunch and the wine were delightful. We went to town and searched for a color TV set like our first one. The small appliance store did not have one. In the bookstore, we bought the *Herald-Tribune* newspaper for the past few days, but there were no new books that interested us.

The movie theater was featuring Jack Lemmon's recent movie *Mister Roberts*, with Henry Fonda, and we decided to see it soon.

The news was dominated by the Civil Rights Movement. Eight black students were denied admission to Sturgis High School in Kentucky. After continued protests, they were admitted.

The supreme court found the Alabama Bus Laws to be unconstitutional. Martin Luther King continued organizing black America throughout the South, and when a problem arose, he marched with the protesters. Television news carefully followed his travels.

In other news, President Eisenhower enacted the Federal Highway Bill, linking forty-one thousand miles across the US. The estimated cost was $25 to $30 billion.

And increased participation by the US military in Vietnam continued to divide the nation as protests continued to increase, sparked by universities across the country. Seemed like the only good news was the rock and roll dance craze sweeping the nation.

September

We celebrated Gina's fiftieth birthday in Ragusa. The drive along the sea was a delight. We sat out on the balcony of our hotel, and I toasted her with a glass of champagne. "Happy birthday, sweetheart."

"Thanks, Giancarlo. I love this place. We need to escape here more often. I pray the tourists fail to discover it. Let them continue flocking like sheep to Taormina."

The sunset highlighted the early evening. It lit up the entire sky with a brilliant orange as it declined to brighten the people in the western part of the world.

When we returned to Siracusa, we saw *Mister Roberts*. It was a comedy-drama aboard a ship as World War II was coming to an end. The cast was led by James Cagney as the commander, Henry Fonda as captain, William Powell as the doctor, and Jack Lemon as an underling laundry steward. Cagney played a crabby, domineering role. Fonda protected Lemon, who always seemed to stumble over himself and was victimized by the commander. As a result, he constantly requested a transfer but was denied. Ultimately Fonda gets transferred and takes Lemon with him and becomes the harsh leader similar to the role played by Cagney.

The film was humorous but was not an epic. It left us in a good mood and relieved our minds of the negative news in the newspaper and on TV.

November

Our return to California was flawless. We slept most of the flight from Rome to New York. Tom and Sandra drove us to the desert and elected to spend the weekend with us.

We went to the club for dinner and caught up on the latest news. President Eisenhower defeated Stevenson in the election. Martin Luther King established his Southern Lutheran Christian Leadership Council in Atlanta, giving him dominance as the leader of the Civil Rights Movement. It loomed over our conversation at dinner.

Sandra said, "Let's change the subject. Why don't we see the movie *Giant* this weekend? It has a cast of the best actors in Hollywood."

We saw it the next evening, and it lived up to the hype it was receiving. Rock Hudson headed the cast with Elizabeth Taylor, James Dean, Rod Taylor, and Mercedes McCambridge. It primarily featured Hudson as a tough headstrong rancher in Texas in the '20s. He ruled over the largest ranch in the state with his newly acquired wife (Taylor). The romance caused conflict with his sister (McCambridge).

It depicted the discrimination and the racist culture against women and Hispanics. The movie was based on a real giant from the nineteenth century named Miguel Ejeicegn. He owned the largest ranch in Texas. He suffered from acromegaly, commonly known as gigantism. He ultimately grew to seven feet, ten inches.

Elvis Presley had become Gina's favorite entertainer, and his earlier recording "Heartbreak Hotel" earned him a spot on the popular *Ed Sullivan Show*. The really big news in the entertainment world was Nat King Cole becoming the first black singer to have his own TV show on prime time.

While watching TV later in the month, we saw disturbing news. A group led by a former Cuban lawyer named Fidel Castro, which included Che Guevara, attempted to land with eighty guerrillas in Havana. Their intent was to overthrow the current leadership, headed by the US-supported regime of Fulgencio Batista, but it was foiled. I commented to Gina, "It seems there's no peace in the world."

Gina replied, "Turn off the TV and stop reading the newspaper. Nothing's new, Giancarlo. Wars and unrest in the world has been going on since Cain and Abel. It's the TV and newspaper media reporting the news in a way we haven't seen before. It's unprecedented."

December

I elected to follow Gina's suggestion—no TV news, no newspaper. Golf and tennis took up our time for most of the month. We did see the movie *The Ten Commandments* with Charlton Heston as Moses and a supporting cast that included Edward G. Robinson and Anne Baxter. It was up for numerous Academy Awards.

We brought in 1957 at Tony and Sharon's house. We had planned on watching the ball drop in Times Square at midnight, but sleep deprived us of the midnight celebration, a relaxing end to an ever-changing year of events.

CHAPTER 14

Palm Springs
January 1957

Cold, damp, cloudy weather opened the new year in the desert. I turned the heat on and made the coffee and turned back to the news-paper. The morning edition highlighted the Civil Rights Movement. The South was rising again, only it was black America, not the plan-tation owners, this time.

Martin Luther King was crisscrossing the country. He was not doing sit-ins at restaurants. He was waking the country up regarding the harsh treatment of his people. His philosophy followed the non-violence doctrine of India's Mahatma Gandhi's approach to indepen-dence from British control. King stressed peaceful demonstrations to arouse America. People of all walks of life were revolting against racism, causing a divide among people and politicians at all levels of government.

I poured a cup of coffee and turned to the business section of the paper. The stock market continued its rise due to the burgeon-ing economy. Automobile sales and new housing construction were leading the way. Inventions of appliances and all furnishings for the home were part of the economic boom. Shopping centers and new schools were being constructed to accommodate suburban housing developments.

Annual income had continued its postwar increases. People were earning more and spending it. The first climate-controlled, totally enclosed mall had opened in Edina, Minnesota. It became a place to shop, dine, and escape the cold, nasty winters of Minneapolis and its suburbs. It featured various forms of entertainment, including a movie theater.

The weather was on my mind. The forecast in the paper for the week was dismal. Rain and cold temperatures meant no golf or tennis.

Gina walked in the den with coffee and kissed the top of my head. "Good morning, Giancarlo. What's with this weather? Will you please wave your magic wand and ask your sun-god friend to wake up. I want to play tennis."

"Good morning, sleepyhead. I hate to be the bearer of bad news. Enjoy the day. It will be the warmest of the week. We need to head to the bookstore and then check out what's playing at the movies."

At the bookstore, a large window displayed Ayn Rand's latest hit book, *Atlas Shrugged*. It was featured on a table at the entrance. Close by, another table promoted Jack Kerouac's *On the Road*. We bought both.

The rain stopped, and we walked to the music store. The window display had a large photo of Frank Sinatra, featuring his latest album *"Where Are You?"* We bought it and also purchased Ella Fitzgerald's "Mack the Knife," Ray Charles's "I Got a Woman," and Gina forced me to buy Little Richard's "Long Tall Sally." Miles Davis's "Round About Midnight" topped the list.

The rain returned, ending our shopping spree. Gina scanned the entertainment section of the newspaper and selected two movies for us to see—*The Three Faces of Eve* with Joanne Woodward and *The Bridge on the River Kwai*, featuring William Holden, Alec Guinness, and a cast of British and Japanese actors. "Let it rain, Giancarlo. We have enough to keep us entertained for the week."

"I have a few other ideas to keep you entertained."

She ignored me.

We received a cable from Salvatore in the afternoon with news from Lucca, covering the status of things in Italy. He reported business was running ahead of the previous year. Major reorders continued from all the distributors, specifically from those where we were doing TV advertising. He voiced concern that if business in the

States followed with increased sales as in Italy, we could have problems supplying everyone.

My thoughts switched to the call I had received from Evan regarding the Spanish olive oil. I cabled Salvatore back, asking for the results of testing that oil. I was eager to get his reply.

Gina suggested we go to the club for dinner. Sharon Bomaritto saw us and invited us to join her and Tony. I discussed the Spanish olive situation with Tony and asked if he had been approached by any of his purveyors to try it. He said he had not, but Sharon said she saw it displayed at Ralph's supermarket. I related that we were testing it for content.

Tony said, "Giancarlo, I understand your concern. Allow me to make an observation. I keep an eye on all competition in my business. It includes my restaurant. We have two things to sell: good food at reasonable prices, and we pride ourselves on our service. We feature a quarter-pound hamburger using in-house ground chuck, 100 percent choice beef.

During the last two years, some guy from Chicago named Ray Kroc started opening these self-serve hamburger restaurants called McDonald's. It's similar to In-N-Out. The price of a burger is fifteen cents. We can't compete with that. My meat for our burger costs fifteen cents. I can't be concerned, but In-N-Out has to be concerned. He is their competition!"

My point is you have to compare apples to apples. If the Spanish oil is as good or better than yours, you might have a problem. However, if there's no comparison, keep doing what you're doing."

I mentally recorded Tony's message. Emerson came to mind: *What fears we have endured that failed to arrive.*

Salvatore's cable echoed. Sales in Italy were running ahead of the previous year due to advertising. That was the key. I thought about Marco Pelligrino's suggestion about creating a TV commercial with a woman adding a few drops of oil in a pan and frying something with it. That was an idea I needed to explore.

The four of us went to see *The Three Faces of Eve*. Lee J. Cobb was Joanne Woodward's costar, along with Alistair Cooke. Woodward's role was a woman plagued with severe headaches and blackouts. She sought the aid of a psychiatrist (Cobb). He was stunned and struggled to find a solution to the cause of her problems. He hypnotized her, and under hypnosis, she turned into three different personalities. Her three names changed, as did her demeanor. He continued to struggle to find a solution. He could not figure out which personality would show up once she was hypnotized.

Cobb took her back to early childhood, and the third personality surfaced and confronted the childhood where her problems began. After additional therapy, she was dramatically cured. The movie highlighted alternative therapies for dealing with mental illness, a growing concern in our culture.

We returned to our house, and Gina cooked some pasta with her marinara sauce for dinner with Tony and Sharon. I put the Sinatra album on while Tony opened a bottle of wine.

Sinatra's current struggles with his estranged wife Ava Gardner were in the tabloid news. The paparazzi hounded the couple. They had been together for six years. They loved hard and fought hard, often in public. Ava was avoiding him, and Sinatra was having trouble dealing with it. Sharon commented, "Sinatra is getting what he deserved. He was fooling around openly with her while he was married to Nancy, his first wife."

Gina added, "She is no better than he is. She uses men like toilet paper. When she's finished with them, she flushes them down the drain. Look at her past marriages, first to Mickey Rooney, who was at the peak of his career. He helped her get her first movie role. While married to him, she got involved with bandleader Artie Shaw and flushed Rooney down the drain and married Shaw. Then she divorced him and climbed the Hollywood celebrity ladder and married Frank. They deserve each other."

I looked at Tony and asked, "Tony, do you have anything to add about what was said?"

"I would not utter the slightest comment, only that I'm sure there were moments when Frank had a good time."

Sharon said, "What you mean, Mr. Bomaritto, is they enjoyed their time in bed because men like to fantasize what it must be like."

I said, "Tony, do you have anything to say to that?"

Tony said, "Gina, this marinara is the best you have ever served. How about the recipe. I'd like to use it at the restaurant."

Gina was next. "Tony, you are dancing. Are you going to comment on Sharon's statement?"

He remained silent. We had a good laugh. The Sinatra story, the good food, and the wine climaxed a nice evening with friends.

February

Gina and I celebrated my fifty-seventh birthday quietly at home. She made lasagna Bolognese. I lit candles for the table and opened a bottle of amarone. We listened to Ella Fitzgerald, Miles Davis, and Ray Charles. She served baked Alaska with a birthday candle and sang "Happy Birthday." It climaxed a romantic, memorable birthday. I kept the problems of the world and the olive oil business at bay.

Gina asked if I planned anything special for the 225th anniversary of Lucca Olive Oil. "I am thinking of bringing Nancy, Evan, and Brock to party with Anna and the crew in Lucca to celebrate. What do you think?"

She said, "You should invite the Italian distributors and the US distributors too."

I liked that idea and decided to put it in motion. That same day, I began inviting people and received enthusiastic replies.

March

The negative news from Vietnam and the Civil Rights Movement continued to top the TV networks. As reported in the national news, a black woman named Rosa Parks in Montgomery, Alabama, refused to give up her seat to a white woman on a bus. The bus driver had her arrested, inciting protests for the rest of the month and boycotts of white businesses for two weeks.

The South Vietnam government was besieged by insurgent opposition, threatening to overthrow it. Terrorist attacks by the insurgents and security forces were clashing. Word leaked that the US was spending $187 million for arms supplies and the salaries of the South

Vietnam military. This widened the division of the American people about the war.

April

We arrived in Lucca in favorable weather. We informed Anna and Salvatore of the planned party for the end of the month. Salvatore and I began calling the Italian distributors while Gina made hotel reservations for those attending the weekend celebration.

The next day, Salvatore, Giuseppe, and I reviewed the tests on the Spanish olive oil and found it had been slightly diluted with vegetable oil. However, the blend was well done. The flavor was not nearly the quality of our oil. I asked Anna to fry some meat in it, and it did not taste very good. Gina made an interesting comment after tasting the fried meat. "Giancarlo, look at this from the viewpoint of a lady on a budget shopping at Ralph's grocery stores. The price is 30 percent less than our oil. That woman is not going to shop at the Italian specialty store. She is not our customer."

"You're correct, Gina, but we need to stay on top of things." The test results eased my mind, and I learned about the taste when it's used for frying. This convinced me not to be concerned about it.

"With the upcoming celebration, what menus are you planning with Anna? For dinner Friday night, we have ten distributors plus their wives plus Nancy, Evan, Brock, Anna, Salvatore, Giuseppe, and the thirty field workers, a total of fifty-eight guests. The out-of-town guests will have breakfast at the hotel. That leaves lunch and dinner for Saturday."

"Anna and I have it under control, Giancarlo. You handle the wine."

The weekend was upon us, and we set up a table at the hotel to receive the guests. We served hors d'oeuvres and prosecco as they walked in the door. Salvatore and I made introductions, and the celebration was off to a warm start.

Dinner was served on the patio buffet-style—breaded chicken breast Milanese, salad, and asparagus parmigiana. Baskets of Anna's sliced bread were on each table. Salvatore, Giuseppe, and I circled the tables, pouring local white wine, and the weekend festa began. A gentle breeze kept the evening heat comfortable.

After everyone departed, Gina and I sat on the patio and talked about the past six years. While the small business existed when I inherited it, it was nowhere near what we had built. The disenchanted distributors in Italy had become content, sharing the success we enjoyed. Our six distributors in the States were doing almost as much business as those in Italy. I remarked about the camaraderie shared at dinner between the Italians and those from the US. Fortunately, the Italians all spoke English.

Gina and Anna's lunch the next day featured fried veal baby meatballs, eggplant parmigiana and minisandwiches of tuna salad. We had bottles of wine on the tables. All I could think of was how Anna and Gina could top the two meals for Saturday night's dinner. They did it with ease, and everyone enjoyed that dinner, which surpassed the previous meals. Mini-individual pizzas were served first, followed by small filets with a béarnaise sauce and zucchini slices fried in our oil. When the meat was served, one could hear a pin drop as people began eating.

The guests stayed for a while and began exchanging success stories on business in their respective regions. Salvatore, Giuseppe, and I moved from table to table and listened. We learned a lot from various things they were doing to promote and sell the oil. Most of the success was attributed to Salvatore and Giuseppe's travels with the distributors' salesmen. And in the States, the stories were the same. The work of Nancy, Brock, and Evan was the main contribution to success.

Saying good night, we invited everyone to stay and enjoy the evening. When we got to our room, Gina looked at me and said, "Let's wait another 225 years to do this again."

I smiled and agreed.

Salvatore's statement regarding the potential problem of supplying our distributors plagued my mind. We had no way to determine the yield of the fall harvest. The weather was the determining factor. I decided to call Signore Sapienza, our neighbor to the south, to see if he had sold his property. I wanted the option to buy the harvest in case we needed more olives. I learned that he had sold his fall harvest to some people in Puglia.

Then I made a call to a broker in town, seeking other possible resources, and he said he knew of no one with any olives to sell for the coming harvest. That left me with no alternatives. All we could do is hope for a strong fall harvest.

I met weekly with Salvatore, and we monitored the sales. The reorders from the States and Italy continued to show increases against last year's numbers. Fortunately, we had no problem filling the orders, but inventory continued to concern us. We projected the needs for the five months left in the season based on the current weekly stream of orders. We determined there could be a problem if the increases continued.

I had been thinking of making a trip to Germany to search for a distributor there and also thought about the possibility of South America but decided to put both considerations aside for the time being. I needed to give it all some time to see what transpired.

CHAPTER 15

July

Our trip to Siracusa was the escape I needed. The first six months of the year provided all the stress for the entire year. The Spanish olive oil controversy, the concern about inventory, and all the other troublesome issues were not life-threatening, but I needed to put them to bed. It was our turn to spend some quality time relaxing and reading at our hideaway in Sicily.

I had read about Jack Kerouac and his literary group of friends in an article in the *New York Times*. The group started a movement in the '40s, opposing authority, materialism, and conformity. They were committed to free speech and liberal sex and openly opposed the Vietnam War. They challenged mainstream society. Kerouac dubbed them "the Beat Generation."

I began reading Jack Kerouac's *On the Road*. The plot of the story, while fiction, depicted the main character traveling across the US by bus and hitchhiking. It was based on the true story of Kerouac's personal travel experiences. Those experiences included his exposure to drugs, attraction to jazz music, menial part-time jobs, and the ups and downs of his love life. He met people at all levels of life and became friends with those who understood his thinking.

He spent ten years on the road, during which time, he fought depression and loneliness. During the period, he began writing about his experiences, deleting and rewriting. Finally, with the aid of a friend, he put the story to bed and published the book. It was acclaimed as one of the top one hundred books of the twentieth century.

I took time from reading to keep up with current events. TV news continued to spotlight the war in Vietnam. Eisenhower continued to increase the US military presence. Several American soldiers and officers were killed when a bomb went off at a US headquarters location near the Châu Đốc area.

Then a major event in the news jolted Americans. The USSR launched a satellite called Sputnik into space. It circled the globe and brought on the USSR-US space war. Russia had achieved military technology, scientific research, and an edge against the US, which gave them a political advantage in the world.

In other news, IBM began selling the first personal computer. After reading about it, I sent a cable to Salvatore, and I suggested he get a salesman to come to Lucca to demonstrate computer technology.

The best news was the economy. There was virtually no unemployment.

There was a buzz about a new movie we wanted to see. It was *The Bridge on the River Kwai*. The story begins in a Japanese prisoner of war camp in Thailand in 1943. The prisoners are both American and British.

The camp is under the command of a tough Japanese captain. He orders the prisoners to build a bridge over the river. An American army officer refuses, citing the Geneva Conference rule, stipulating that officers who are prisoners of war were not subjected to manual labor. He is forced to make the officer stand at attention in the hot sun for twenty-four hours and later had him thrown in a cage and beaten. Two of the prisoners escaped while the bridge was under construction.

The Japanese captain was under a strict mandate to complete the bridge by a certain day. A freight train was scheduled to cross between Bangkok and Rangoon with military supplies. A plan by the escaped prisoners and those building the bridge was to blow up the bridge on the scheduled day of arrival by the train.

Meanwhile, the Japanese captain was pushing the prisoners harshly because they were behind schedule. The escaped soldiers returned. Working at night using the moonlight, they began placing sticks of explosives on the bridge's structure the day before the scheduled train arrival. The next morning, they learned the water level had reduced below the structure, exposing the explosives.

As the train was approaching, the Japanese captain pulled one of the wires leading to the detonator and called for the Japanese soldiers to launch grenades at the prisoners. He is attacked and stabbed by a prisoner as a grenade hits the soldier who had the detonator at his feet. The soldier falls on it as the train crosses the bridge. The blast destroys the bridge, and the train falls into the river.

The movie was up for several Academy Awards.

August

I was sitting on the patio, about to begin reading *Atlas Shrugged*, when Alena approached with a cable from Salvatore. My sixth sense signaled bad news, and it was worse than I suspected.

> Giancarlo I am sorry to report, we are getting complaints from the distributors that an inexpensive oil is appearing on the shelves of stores here in Italy. It is labeled olive oil, but it is not, it doesn't even look like olive oil. They are saying some of their purveyors are selling it too. Evan says it is appearing in the U.S. too.

I was shocked. My mind shut down. I could not imagine people producing this garbage could be enjoying the success in both the US and Italy.

Gina joined me, and I handed her the cable. After reading it, the look on her face was total disbelief. She said, "What is wrong with people? How can they do this and get away with it?"

"It's greed, Gina. It's quick money. They are in it to make a fast dollar. They know it will be short-lived. It is only a matter of time. Once the consumer tries it, they will not return to the store and buy it again. By then, the scumbags that are selling it will be off to the next scam to enrich themselves."

"But, Giancarlo, what about the purveyors selling it to the restaurants?"

"They, too, will suffer. Whether they use it to fry or for salads, the customers will revolt and complain."

"There's no integrity, Giancarlo. What are you going to do?"

"Gina, first we need to find out how serious the distribution is. When there's a surprise attack, you have to regroup, devise a plan, and retaliate. My plan is to get with our distributors and those purveyors we can trust and try to find the culprits distributing it. We can no longer wait for the Department of Economic Development to combat these people. Who knows? They may have someone in that department on their payroll."

"But how, Giancarlo? Even if you find them, how do you stop them?"

"What they are doing, Gina, is illegal. They are misrepresenting the product by calling it olive oil. I will be sending a cable to Evan, instructing him to meet with our distributors, seeking information as to who the distributor is and what we can do to put them out of business."

I sent the cables to Salvatore and Evan, advising them to set up group meetings with our distributors. The goal was to use every method available to find the distributors of the phony oil. I said,

> The best approach is to use contacts with
> the purveyors to see if they had been approached.
> Perhaps someone from the phony distributors left
> a name and phone number, or a business card.
> Maybe they left a price list or brochure.

When Gina and I sat down for lunch, I told her, "We need to return to Lucca to work with Salvatore and the distributors. Gina, I can't leave here and return to the States and hope this thing resolves itself. If we allow these people to infiltrate our business, it will be like cancer. It'll spread to every level of our business."

"I agree, Giancarlo. We can leave tomorrow if you want."

"Good. Let's do that."

There seemed to be no end to people trying to bring cheap oil to the market.

Lucca

"Giancarlo, I'm going to draft a letter for our distributors to send to all their customers, warning them of this oil. A simple one-page description of the packaging will let the buyer beware of the fraud."

"Good idea, Gina. It needs to go to the purveyors too. Cable a copy to Evan, Brock, and Nancy."

I called all the distributors and organized a one-day meeting in Firenze for the following week. Salvatore and I went to visit Maria Antinora, our Lucca distributor the next day. "Signora, we are disturbed about the cheap oil that has surfaced recently. Have you been approached?"

She replied, "No, signore, we have not."

I showed her a bottle. She was stunned. "Giancarlo, I can't believe this. Who would be stupid enough to buy it? It doesn't even look like olive oil."

I said, "Signora, you know many people in the business. Please approach your grocery-store clients and purveyors. See if you can find out who is distributing this garbage and get back to us as soon as possible."

"Giancarlo, you have my word. I will be on it the minute you walk out the door. I have a friend in Firenze who is a private investigator. I will engage him to get involved. He's an old family friend and will not charge anything for the service."

We used the same approach with the distributors in Firenze the following week that we used with Signora Antinora. It met with the enthusiasm we had hoped for.

Evan cabled that he and Brock and Nancy were meeting with the US distributors the following week in St. Louis. I cabled back and stated the approach we used with the Italian distributors and advised him to do the same. The retaliation was on.

We decided there was not much left for us to do in Lucca and flew back to Siracusa. When we arrived at the house, Gina said, "Giancarlo, we have had enough stress over this problem. Let the plan work. You need to relax. This was not part of the plan to market the oil."

I took her advice to heart and began relaxing the best way I knew by burying my head in Ayn Rand's book *Atlas Shrugged*. It was so far removed from her earlier books that it was hard to discern it was written by the same author, but as I got into it, I marveled at her versatility. I loved the story.

The story was deemed as a rule of man's mind on existence and philosophical themes and how businesses suffered under the ridiculous laws and regulations. The fictional main character was a female railroad executive who fell in love with a man who was a giant in the steel industry. The novel documented their struggle against those attempting to exploit their respective businesses.

There was no specific time in history in the story, but the US was heading into economic collapse and taking on the appearance of the business disaster of the 1880s. At this point, US society became characterized by human oppression and severe health issues due to squalor and overcrowding. A negative and mysterious figure attempted to overthrow the major businesses and tried to get the leaders to abandon their companies. Strikes and looters prevailed, but in the end, a large group saved the day by succeeding with a new capitalistic society.

The novel was riveting.

*****

Palm Springs
November

Salvatore sent a cable with news that the distributors were beginning to learn of individuals selling the cheap oil but no news on the actual name of the distributor. Those names were sales representatives. I called Evan as soon as we arrived and received similar news.

It was obvious the distributor was smart enough to avoid exposure. Gina urged me to relax, play golf, and enjoy life.

We had Thanksgiving at the club with Sharon and Tony, and the discussion was centered on the cheap oil until Gina put a stop to it. Later at home, she scolded me about it. "Giancarlo, please, I am sick of this obsession you have about the problem."

I had no words to respond and decided to heed her frustration.

December

At breakfast the following week, I listened to Gina's plans for the coming week, which included an invitation from Sandra and Tom to visit Laguna Beach at their house and take a few side trips. I smiled and said, "Sounds good to me. What other plans do you have for the rest of the month?"

"Are you being obstinate, Mr. Giambrone?"

Laughing, I said, "No, ma'am, I am relying on you for entertainment for the rest of the year. No way do I want to spend time in the institution to which you have banished me in the past, as much as I enjoy puppies."

"That's better, sweetheart."

"Oh, so now it's sweetheart. I like that better"

"Careful there. You're treading on thin ice."

We had a great time traveling up and down the Pacific coast highway with Sandra and Tom, stopping in historic San Clemente, Carlsbad, and a weekend in La Jolla. It was a good tonic escaping from the hectic past three months.

They insisted we spend the Christmas and New Year holidays with them—icing on the cake. It was a nice retreat. The casual lifestyle of Southern California with no obligations for the last two weeks of 1957 were the best of the year.

CHAPTER 16

Palm Springs
January 1958

I awoke to a beautiful, sunny day eager to learn more about the bogus olive oil. A cable arrived from Salvatore with the analysis of the phony oil. Some bottles had a mixture of oils that included canola, peanut, and vegetable oil and an unknown green powder. Others had a combination of vegetable, corn, and soybean oil, again with an unknown green substance. But the distribution source continued to be a mystery. This was not the news I was hoping for. Our US distributors were using all their resources at all levels to find the origin of distribution and with no success.

At breakfast, Gina did her best to ease my distress over the matter. The fact remained it was appearing more and more in certain purveyors' warehouses and restaurants. In addition, we learned Spanish olive oil was being used by some of the smaller restaurants. The good news was we were holding our own in the States and doing better in Italy. It was obvious the Italians were more discerning and inclined to use the real thing.

Gina and I divided the morning newspaper. The front page was almost exclusively centered on Vietnam. North Vietnam sent a newly organized, well-trained group called the Vietcong deep into South Vietnam. It consisted of 1,700 men who were well equipped and supplied by China. They immediately made serious advances and surprised the south military and the US advisors.

Meanwhile, the north communist leaders met with a South Vietnam group of insurgents in an attempt to organize free elections in the fall. The plot was to stage an uprising on the Diệm government. A report surfaced that the South Vietnam government had little or no support in many of the remote areas throughout the south. These were easy targets for the North Vietnamese military to take control of.

In other news, a book was released called *The Ugly American*, written by Eugene Burdick and William Lederer. With its scathing picture of US State Department personnel, it hit the *New York Times* bestseller list. The *Saturday Evening Post* magazine ran a series of it, and the masses in America were reading it, causing more disdain for the war. The plot was modeled after a former CIA agent who had gained the confidence of South Vietnam president Diệm so that he could spy on the regime.

Gina read the entertainment section and commented on movies we should see. They included *Gigi* with French actors Leslie Caron, Maurice Chevalier, Louis Jordan, and American Eva Gabor. A second was with David Niven, *Separate Tables*. Both movies were up for several Academy Awards.

She also shared news of a credit card, the first called BankAmericard, subtitled VISA, issued by Bank of America. It was available for use everywhere in all businesses with terms for payment monthly or with a minimum payment with interest charges.

In the business section, a new invention, an automatic washing machine, was a main topic of interest. The report stated there was a waiting list to get one.

The most exciting item was an article about Texas Instruments scientist Jack Kirby, who invented the first integrated circuit, which revolutionized the electronics industry. It was a microchip made up of multiple components for use in computers, telephones, and TV sets. Its various functions included processing and storing information. It sounded like an historic game changer.

Later in the morning, I placed a call to the advertising agency in LA and gave them a budget for initiating the billboard ads across the country, including St. Louis, Chicago, Boston, Atlanta, and Dallas. In addition, I authorized them to begin showing twenty-second TV commercials on the six-o'clock and ten-o'clock news in LA.

With the sunny and warm weather, we put business and the news of the day aside. Gina went to play tennis, and I escaped to the golf course.

February

Gina invited Sandra, Tom, Sharon, and Tony to the house to celebrate my fifty-eighth birthday. And after dinner, we watched the Academy Awards, hosted by Bob Hope, Jack Lemon, Jimmy Stewart, and David Niven. The movie winners were *Gigi*, best movie; David Niven, best actor; with Susan Hayward, best actress. Winners for supporting roles were Wendy Hiller and Burl Ives.

After the awards, Gina brought a beautiful cake with one birthday candle, and the group sang "Happy Birthday." Sandra asked, "Well, Giancarlo, do you have words of wisdom to share with us tonight about turning fifty-eight?"

"I do, Sandra. It is about the four letter-word *time*. We take it for granted as children. We don't think about how precious it is. We can't wait to arrive at the stations. We want life to hurry, rushing to graduate from grade school to get to high school. The goal to reach sixteen is the next push to get our driver's license. Twenty-one is the next station, reaching legal age. We want to finish our education and get on with a career and make money to buy all those material things we had dreamed about, including that first fancy car. *Time* is not on the mind.

"We waste *time*. How many times has someone asked, 'Let's meet for a meal,' and your reply is, 'I don't have time'? We crowd our schedule with so many nonsensical, time-consuming things that are not important.

"We marry and soon get into a routine that involves a schedule so loaded, we forget to 'take time' to do the little things that originally brought us together. We are too busy.

"Meanwhile the clock is ticking, and one day, we reach an age and begin to wonder, 'Where did the *time* go?' We realize we're running out of *time*. Think about it: all the money in the world can't buy one minute."

Tom said, "Giancarlo, you never cease to amaze me with your philosophy about life. I have no idea where it comes from, but that lesson just woke me up. I am sure I speak for everyone at this table, we just went back to school. Thank you for sharing. Happy birthday, my friend."

March

Gina and I went to Downtown Palm Springs, to visit an indoor shopping mall celebrating its grand opening. The top LA stores opened branches. There was a movie theater featuring *Gigi*, and we attended the matinee. It was a musical comedy. Louis Jordan played the role of a wealthy Parisian playboy who didn't work. He moved from mistress to mistress and lived a luxurious lifestyle. He was handsome and had a reputation as a ladies' man. Gigi was played by Leslie Caron, who was sent by her mother to Paris to live with a former mistress to learn manners and etiquette and to experience the way of life of a mistress.

The aunt introduced Gigi to Gaston (Louis Jordan). The plan was for him to show her the lifestyle of living in Paris and groom her to be a mistress. The early part of their time together was platonic, but Gaston falls in love. The aunt sees his attraction, and she proposes to Gigi to be his mistress, but Gigi shuns the idea.

As time goes by, Gaston pleads with Gigi and tells her of his love. Again, she refuses. Soon, she realizes she too, is in love. Gaston approaches the aunt and asks for her hand in marriage. They ultimately marry. It was a romantic comedy for the ages.

After the movie, we shopped at the bookstore. We bought *Doctor Zhivago* by Russian author Boris Pasternak. Next, we shopped for music. We bought Sinatra's *Come Fly with Me*, James Brown's "I Got You (I Feel Good)," Count Basie and Joe Williams's "One for My Baby (and One More for the Road)" and the new duo the Everly Brothers' "All I Have to Do Is Dream."

Protests against the war in Vietnam continued to divide the nation. Opposition mounted between those protesting and those who felt the communist government of North Vietnam needed to be stopped. They felt the protesters were unpatriotic. Organized clashes occurred at the protests, bringing police forces to separate and control the crowds. The bad news spread across the world, and America was accused of trying to be the world's police force. The divide between the US and the Russian and Chinese forces grew wider. Politicians in Congress began fighting openly about their opinions about America's involvement, many calling for withdrawal.

There was an economic element in the picture. Congressmen from states producing materials for the war were opposed to ending it, for obvious reasons. It was fueling their economies.

Meanwhile, the conservative media severely criticized President Eisenhower for his continued support and sending more American soldiers to the cause. He sent an additional two thousand men to the conflict. The war weighed heavily on Americans.

The country was divided on two fronts—the war in Vietnam and the Civil Rights Movement.

*****

Lucca
April

The arrival at our villa provided the escape from the war news but not the issues with our business. I felt the weight of the world had been lifted. I was against the war. The only peace the country enjoyed were the four years between the end of World War II and the Korean conflict. It bothered me that I could no longer discuss Vietnam with business associates. It was too controversial.

We were invited to a meeting in Milan with a group of food manufacturers. The agenda included product labeling with regard to content. A petition was circulated to present to the Italian government, citing examples of fraud, including the fake olive oil.

Representatives from San Marzano attended, showing cans of tomatoes, claiming they were grown in San Marzano, but proof was displayed that they were from Sicily. That remained in my mind. Could our culprit selling fake oil be from Sicily?

When we returned to Lucca, Maria Antinora, our distributor, referred me to her private investigator, and I called him. After our introduction, I asked if he had a contact in the export department in Sicily. I shared my suspicion that the source for distribution to the US was emanating from there. He said, "Signore, I don't have a contact, but I have a friend with the Italian export department in Milan who will seek the information in Sicily."

That was a start and I awaited the next step.

May

We needed some new scenery, so we decided to go to San Remo on the Italian riviera. The drive along the Tyrrhenian Sea was breathtaking. The water was like glass. Hardly a wave could be seen because there was no wind. The reflection from the sun on the water was like looking into a mirror. Gina asked, "Giancarlo, please pull over so we can walk the beach."

We removed our sneakers, rolled up our pant legs, and walked, allowing the warm surf to rinse the sand off our feet and ankles. We didn't talk. I thought of my recent birthday party and the discussion about *time*. It was sharing moments like this with Gina that made me happy. Doing the things with her that brought us together in the early days had been missing. I chastised myself. Politics, the news, the business, and my sometimes-selfish life had consumed precious time. I was guilty of violating my own philosophy.

I decided to sell the olive oil business—the business but not the land. It was not a coincidence that Gina had asked to walk the beach. I reminded myself there is no such thing as coincidence. This was meant to be.

We stopped in Forte dei Marmi for lunch at Osteria del Mare. Our table was on the edge of the sand. Gina was facing the sea and the bright sun. I stared at her while she was looking at the menu. Her beauty and the moment were another nail in the coffin of the olive oil business. All I needed was a plan for the sale. I thought about the employees at every level, and the pressure considering their future was already mounting. Out of consideration for the rest of the trip, I put it out of my mind.

Gina rescued me with her lunch decision. We satisfied our appetites and were back on the road.

San Remo

We checked in to Nyala Hotel. Our suite faced the sea, and the balcony provided a picturesque view of the city. A bottle of prosecco was on ice, and a bowl of fresh fruit was on the table. A plate with three cheeses completed the warm greeting.

We watched the fading sunset and enjoyed the wine, fruit, and cheese. Again, *time* entered my mind. We need to do more of this.

The hotel provided a brochure with the monthly events scheduled and a brief history of the city, which dated back to the early Roman days. A photo of a thirteenth-century church was highlighted, along with photos of a beautiful Japanese garden. It spoke of an annual music festival to be held toward the end of the month.

After feasting on the gratuitous food provided in the room, we walked the area around the hotel. The palm-tree-lined streets with nicely dressed people speaking Italian resembled a Rembrandt painting. They were locals, not American tourists. I said to Gina, "This is our new hideaway. Let's avoid exposing this city to the world. I do not want what has happened to Positano to happen here. The crowds in Positano now resemble amusement parks in the US."

Our dinner was at Fior d'Italia, one of the oldest restaurants in the city. The menu had a few pasta selections for starters. The main courses were seafood. When the waiter presented our selection, a whole sea bass was twitching, alive, taking its final breaths. The food and service were superb, and we made reservations for our second night.

On our return, we spent the weekend in Forte dei Marmi at the Hotel St. Mauritius and had dinner at Lorenzo.

May

Back in Lucca, a cable from Evan greeted me the first thing Monday morning. Sam Marzullo, our distributor in California, had a lead on a local LA importer selling both the Spanish olive oil and also the fake oil. One of his top purveyors was approached by a woman attempting to sell both oils to him.

In an effort to trap her, he bought some of both, took her to lunch, and after a couple glasses of wine, secured the name of her company and the owner. Sam approached the authorities at US customs with the information, along with the fake bottle of olive oil. Through computer research, they found the receiving documents revealing the shipment's country of origin. It was Sicily—no surprise to me. Sam was promised that an investigation would take place. I immediately called the import authorities in Milan to pass the California importer's name and his company.

When Gina joined me for breakfast, I explained what had happened. "Giancarlo, at the risk of you calling me an alarmist, I am scared. This is another case of Mafia involvement."

"Gina, the Mafia is involved mostly in legal undertakings, including production of olive oil. I am sure it is a group of small-time idiots trying to make a quick buck."

"Giancarlo, your mind is so cluttered with so many things. You're not thinking the way I am. So how about this idea: call the private investigator in Firenze and ask him to use his sources in Sicily to check with the grocery stores to see if they are selling the fake oil. If so, it is hurting the regular olive oil business controlled by the mob. If the Sicilian authorities don't put a halt to the bandits selling the fake oil, I pity those bandits. The Mafia will handle the problem once they become aware of the infractions on their business. The bandits will disappear."

Smiling, I got up from my chair and went over and gave her a warm good morning embrace and squeezed her tightly. She responded with a mouth-to-mouth kiss and said, "I love you, handsome."

"I love you too, sweetheart. Let's have some breakfast."

After breakfast, I made the call to the investigator in Firenze and asked him to check with his contacts in Sicily regarding Gina's suggestion. I had to remind myself of *time*. I kept vacillating back and forth on the activity with the authorities in LA, those in Milan, and the private investigator's work in progress in Sicily.

May

The rain came with a heavy pour. Thunderstorms struck and continued through the night. It did not let up for three days. Salvatore and Giuseppe split the field workers into two groups to drive their three-wheeled vehicles across the entire area to see if the trees had been damaged. At the end of the day, he reported minor problems had been found, and the trees were trimmed of dead limbs.

Meanwhile, we were locked indoors. I had commented to Gina how grateful I was that this was not happening in August and September, for it could ruin the harvest or certainly have serious effects on it.

The morning newspaper, as in the past, focused on the war. A US diplomat named Elbridge Durbrow voiced a severe negative assessment of Ngô Đình Diệm, the president of South Vietnam. It spoke of continued disruption of his government by insurgents and his overall lack of control of the war efforts by the South Vietnam military. Durbrou's critique zeroed in on the waste of US money.

After the Japanese departed Vietnam at the end of World War II, the French continued fighting Ho Chi Minh's guerrillas. President Harry Truman began supplying the French. Durbrou stated,

> The U.S. has been pouring American taxpayers hard earned money down the drain. God only knows where those billions of dollars ended up. There was not a shred of success while the French were there, and the same conditions have prevailed since the American military entered the scene.

Amen to that.

We had had enough of the rain and flew to Catania and the sunshine of Sicily and enjoyed the nice, warm breeze along the ocean on the way to Siracusa.

CHAPTER 17

Siracusa
July

I began reading Boris Pasternak's *Doctor Zhivago*. When I read the review in the *New York Times*, I learned it had been banned in Russia. The censors felt it was anti-Soviet. Pasternak had major concerns about the lifestyle and welfare of the Russian people and criticized former dictator Joseph Stalin. Someone smuggled the book to Milan, and it was published, to the dismay of Soviet officials.

The story begins at the turn of the twentieth century in Russia as the czarist control declines, and the revolution is under way. The main characters are Dr. Yuri Zhivago; Tanya, his first wife; a beautiful young Lara; a young man named Pasha, who falls in love with Lara and marries her; and a tough Russian general named Kamarovsky.

Young Lara is raped by her mother's lover, military general Victor Kamarovsky, and her life's struggles begin. Her mother learns of the rape and attempts suicide. Lara, despondent over the general's constant mistreatment of her, stalks him and follows him to a party.

Dr. Zhivago is at the party, now married to Tanya. Lara attempts to kill the general and shoots him in the arm and faints. Dr. Zhivago initially tries to aid Lara and is amazed at her beauty but quickly moves to aid the general. Pasha, also in attendance, escorts Lara safely away while the general is being helped. Pasha begins seeing Lara and later marries her.

Yuri is drafted into the Russian Army as a battlefield doctor when World War I breaks out. Pasha joins the war effort and becomes missing in action and presumed dead. Lara, now a nurse in the war, meets Yuri, and working together, they fall in love, but Yuri remains faithful to Tanya.

After Russia exits the war, a group of anticommunist forces begin fighting the Bolsheviks. They capture Yuri, who later escapes and disappears for two years. Lara spends a great deal of time searching for him, as does his wife Tanya. Tanya is aware they both are searching for Yuri.

Lara and Yuri reunite and secretly move to a hideaway on the outskirts of Moscow. Soviet police are searching for Yuri. A friend alerts them and offers to get them out of the country. Initially, they refuse, but Yuri later convinces Lara to leave with the promise that he will follow later, but he fails to do so. He later moved to Moscow, and, living alone, had a heart attack and died.

Lara learns of his death and returns for his funeral. She convinces Yuri's half brother to help her search for a lost daughter she had conceived with Yuri. Soviet authorities discover she is back in town and arrest her, and she disappears. It is believed she is arrested during Joseph Stalin's great purge and later becomes a nameless number on a list later misplaced.

I really enjoyed this epic novel.

At the bookstore, Gina purchased a book on the history of olive oil and its uses around the world. She made notes as she read and learned as far back as five thousand years in Crete, olive oil was used for soap, medicine, and as a moisturizer.

Archaeologists discovered its usage by the Minoans for soap. The use for cosmetics there dated back to the seventh century BC. Trade between Egypt and Crete became the source of wealth for the producers. The Egyptians used it for soap and in cosmetics for moisturizing their bodies. Gina shared her notes with me and was determined to get the Milan companies to begin using our oil to produce soap and develop cosmetics.

The TV news switched from the war to the US recession that began in the late summer of 1957. It was the third postwar period of economic decline. Blame was put on the Asian flu epidemic, which killed eighty thousand people before it was brought under control. That caused a decline in the labor pool, which hurt production of most commodities. Shortage prevailed, and the age-old supply-and-demand imbalance caused inflation. That prompted the Federal Reserve to raise interest rates. Thus, the money source dried up. Higher interest rates slowed the sale of homes and automobiles. Those industries controlled as much as 15 to 20 percent of the American labor force. Unemployment rose to 7.8 percent.

As in the past, the Fed caused the recession, now in its eighth month. Then the Fed lowered the rate charged to banks to 1.75 percent. And as the historical past repeats itself, the economy now was beginning to reverse itself.

*****

September

Rain began falling early in the month. It was not a normal fall storm. We had never experienced anything like that. News on TV showed it covering all of Italy, stretching across lower Europe. It continued for the rest of the week.

Alarmed, I called Salvatore and asked how badly it was affecting the harvest. "Signore, we are not able to do anything. The rain has kept us inside. However, it is early. Before the rain started, we had checked the olives, and they had not reached maturity. If the rain stops in the next two or three days, we will be fine. There is nothing we can do at this point. I will keep you posted. Relax and enjoy Siracusa."

The rain did not stop. It got worse and now covered all of Europe. The heaviest storms were in the south. Salvatore called, and the tone of his voice was all I needed to hear. He told me they had no choice but to harvest the olives in the rain. It was too early to tell what effect the rain had on the crop. The crewmen were worn out. Some were sick and needed medical attention. Only half the workforce was available.

I tried my best to prop up Salvatore, but his mind was on the harvest. He was more concerned than I was. I began thinking about the possibility of a shortfall should production go below our needs to supply our distributors.

When Gina heard the news, her mind began working overtime, listening to the woes but seeking a solution at the same time. "Giancarlo, how many times in your life have you faced possible disasters, only to find they did not become as disruptive as you feared?"

I looked at her and shook my head. "Gina, you always do it. I have been consumed by this rain from the first day, and you show up with Emerson's philosophy and ease the pain."

"Let's go into town and have a nice lunch and share a bottle of wine. The entire matter is out of our hands."

The rain slowed the next two days. I did not hear from Salvatore. That was good news. Knowing him, he would have called if trouble persisted.

By midmonth, my anxiety got the better of me, and I waited until the end of the day to call him. "Signore, I apologize for not calling you. We have been working ten- to twelve-hour days, even Sundays. We needed to dry the olives in the warehouse before pressing them. I brought in electric heaters and slowly dried them. I estimate we will probably achieve 80 percent of last year's yield."

I congratulated and thanked him and told him to pay the crew time and a half for the previous two weeks.

*****

Palm Springs
October

I was mentally exhausted when we arrived. We were greeted by warm weather and a gentle breeze. After the rain we had dealt with, it was great to see the sun. I received a cable from Salvatore, stating that his 80 percent projection was close, and he requested a plan for the coming year's distribution.

I cabled back and asked him to do a monthly analysis of sales to each distributor from October of 1957 through August 1958. Once that was completed, he was to project 80 percent of those amounts for the coming year for each client.

I asked Gina to draft a letter to each distributor and advise them that they would be limited to 80 percent of last year's orders and further explain the conditions that caused the dilemma, and extend our apology.

I continued to struggle with my decision to find an easy solution for selling the business. I wanted to formulate the plan before discussing it with Gina. There was no doubt she would oppose it. She was an intricate part of it and seemed to enjoy it. The thought was still in my head as she walked in the room.

The phone rang. Tony wanted me to join him on the golf course. He rescued me. He and I had lunch after our golf game, and I decided to confide in him and told him my plan to sell the business.

"Giancarlo, you have loyal, honest, hardworking, dedicated employees to think about. I know you well enough they weigh heavy on your mind. You have built a successful team. What are your plans for them? A prospective buyer will be very concerned about them. Will they stay? That buyer will want you to stay on during a transitional period because you and Gina are part of the team. Are you willing to acquiesce? Have you arrived at a price? Do the olive groves go with the business? Is the villa in Lucca part of the package? And lastly, what's your time frame?"

"Wow, Tony, I have been so preoccupied with the thought of selling it, I haven't taken the time to think of all these questions."

We reviewed the issues again, and I wrote them down.

It was time to meet with Gina and discuss the sale. My notes from lunch with Tony provided the strength to break the news to her. I was prepared for her surprise and negative reaction. "Gina, I have made a decision to sell the olive oil business. Please listen before you respond.

It has reached a point where it's no longer fun. The stress and day-to-day responsibilities have begun to interfere with our lives. Soon, I will be turning sixty years old, and it has dawned on me that I have been on this earth longer than I have time left to enjoy it. The two most precious four-letter words—*life* and *time*—have brought me to this decision. I have a plan that Tony and I put together this afternoon. I want to share it with you.

"Wow, Giancarlo, this is a shock. When did you decide this?"

"I have been thinking about it for some time and made the final decision while we were walking the beach in San Remo."

"I don't know what to say. However, I am a little surprised you met with Tony before telling me of your decision."

"It was not preplanned, sweetheart. It surfaced in a casual conversation. I wanted an opinion from someone who was not connected to the business."

"Giancarlo, there are a lot of people depending on your leadership. They have dedicated their time and effort to make the company a success. Who will replace you? I am sure you have thought about it. What's the plan?"

"First of all, let's table my replacement for a minute. My plan is to spend the next year preparing for the eventual sale. The sale will be for the business, not the land and olive groves. There will be two divisions under one heading, one in Italy and the other in the US.

I will offer Italy to Salvatore and Giuseppe and the US to Nancy, Evan, and Brock as owners. Thus, the five of them will be partners, owning 20 percent each. We will form a new corporation selling the assets for a yet-to-be-determined price. We will allow them to pay us 20 percent each year over a five-year period. We will not charge them interest, which is a reward for their hard work and dedication you mentioned.

I intend to reach out to Jimmy Boscamp at Bank of America to secure a line of credit for them. Evan will be copresident of the US, and Salvatore will be copresident in Italy.

While we are here, I will immediately begin training Evan on his new role. And next April, when we return to Lucca, I will spend three months training Salvatore. We will hire someone in the US as comptroller to handle financial matters." I turned to Gina for her reaction.

"Giancarlo, I should have known better than to challenge you earlier. That is so typical of how your brain works. I love it. When do you plan to break the news?"

"I am going to have a conference call with the US group immediately, and I will be sending a cable to Salvatore and Giuseppe today."

"Good. I like it. Let's do it, Giancarlo. I think it is good for
both of us, lifting the stress off your head, and it gives us time to
watch more sunsets and walk more beaches. Let me give you a hug,
handsome."

"Is that all I get?"

"Write that cable and make those phone calls, wild man."

*****

The long-distance operator set up a conference call with Nancy,
Brock, and Evan, and I started the meeting. "Good morning, every-
body. Allow me to preface the reason for this call. What I am about
to share is a decision that has taken serious consideration and a plan
that includes the three of you. Don't be shocked. I have decided to
sell the business."

I paused for that to sink in. No one said a word. Then I explained
the plan and solicited their responses.

"Giancarlo, this is Nancy. I am not the least surprised at this
decision. I have often wondered why you spent time building the
business, considering the lifestyle you and Gina have. It never made
sense. That being said, I am grateful of your incredible offer to the
three of us. It is typical Giancarlo Giambrone. You had the option to
sell it to some large firm for a lot of money and receive the sale proceeds immediately without having to wait five years. I am on board,
and rest assured I will continue to dedicate my life to the business."

Evan was next. "Giancarlo, I echo what Nancy just said. I thank
you for the role you have given me, and I assure you, I will never
abuse my authority in any way. I too will continue my dedication to
Lucca Olive Oil."

Brock, laughing, said, "Well, what those two just reiterated
leaves no words for me to add. Include me in. When do you want to
start this, Giancarlo?"

"Once I get the nod from Salvatore and Giuseppe, I intend to
have my attorney put the legal documents together immediately. I

will keep you apprised of the day-to-day activities. Finding the right chief financial officer is my next priority. Be on the lookout in your respective areas for someone."

I formulated the cable and sent it to Salvatore and asked him to discuss it with Giuseppe.

That afternoon, Gina and I went into town and had lunch at Melvin's. I shared the conversation with her about the call with Evan, Brock, and Nancy, with emphasis on Nancy's response.

"Bravo, Giancarlo, that's a good start. Those kids are young, single, and full of energy. There's no doubt in my mind, after a year in their new responsibilities with your training, things will proceed as in the past."

November

Two days later, I received the response from Salvatore. I could sense his elation. It brought a smile to my face. It assured me I had made the right decision. This was not just selling a business; it was achieving two things: first, leaving the 225-year-old business in the hands of family members as opposed to selling it to a large firm. I also felt like I was making a contribution to society because the decision included the field workers, the distributors, their employees, and the employees of their clients.

Salvatore's expression of gratitude brought a tear to my eye, and when Gina read it she, too, showed emotion. It was *time* to relax and enjoy the desert's warm, peaceful climate, to share precious moments with our friends and enjoy life.

The holidays were approaching, and we planned to spend them together, sharing time in Laguna Beach with Sandra and Tom and in Beverly Hills with Sharon and Tony. We had dinner on New Year's Eve at the club, and I broke the news about selling the business and shared the progress with the group.

Shortly before midnight, we hugged and kissed. The year 1958 was history.

CHAPTER 18

Palm Springs
January 1959

America woke up on New Year's Day to startling news. Fidel Castro and his revolutionary army had overthrown the socialist government of Cuba, starting a revolution. The former Cuban attorney, having lost the battle in the Cuban courts in 1952, decided the only way to get rid of the Batista regime was by military force, and in 1953, he fomented his plan.

Castro's troops had taken control of the area in the outskirts of Havana earlier. Batista managed to escape with his family the evening of the invasion. Castro's forces celebrated in the streets of Havana with no retaliation from the Cuban military. Thus began his following of the Marxist-Leninist lines of communism. Cuba became known as the Communist Party of Cuba.

The revolution had international repercussions, especially in the US. The Castro government began to nationalize everything, including the press. It also began intervention in the affairs in Latin America, Africa, Asia, and the Middle East.

Resenting US aid and support for the Batista regime, Castro nationalized US businesses and assets. In turn, President Eisenhower froze Cuban assets and severed diplomatic ties with Cuba. He placed embargoes and sanctions on Cuba, and the divide between the two countries widened.

At breakfast that morning, with Sharon and Tony, we discussed the fact that Castro was not a communist. He was a well-educated, liberal Cuban. His law degree enabled him to sue the government to no avail. He traveled to Russia for support, both financial and military aid. As part of the deal, he promised the authorities he would follow the principles of Lenin if he was successful in overthrowing the Batista regime. It was well known that the Russians had backed his movement.

Sharon asked, "How could our government, knowing the Batista regime was maligning the Cuban people, continue to aid him? Is there any doubt he pocketed a great deal of the money we poured into his hands? If the four of us knew what was going on, how could the CIA and the heads of state just sit back and allow Russia to back this guy? Why didn't the CIA take him out?"

I smiled and said, "Sharon, you and I are in agreement. There are many answers to your many questions. You have to consider the fact US companies were doing a lot of business there. Cuba was dependent on the US for many products, including building materials, automobiles, and military equipment. Lobbyists in DC were feeding congressmen's campaigns. The wealthy Cuban merchants, businesses, and politicians did not want US intervention. It was laissez-faire. It was business as usual. don't fix what's working." That ended the disturbing conversation.

In brighter news, Alaska became the forty-ninth state of America.

Back at home, the real news was a cable from Salvatore.

> Giancarlo, our government intercepted a shipment at the docks in Palermo of the fake olive oil, and arrested an employee signing the shipping documents. He was offered immunity if he agreed to testify against the perpetrators, and he agreed. The factory for the phony oil is in Casteldaccia, twenty-one kilometers from Palermo. Our government forces immediately raided the facility and arrested the people, and an investigation is underway. They seized all the equipment and records.

I read the cable again. It was hard to believe the nightmare was over. Gina walked in as I was pouring a cup of coffee, and I handed it to her. "You're not going to believe this."

She read the cable and said, "Well Giancarlo, another worry has passed. Now all you have to do is figure out how to slow down the Spanish olive oil distribution."

"Gina, I am not that concerned about that situation. It will level off. The better restaurants will not use it, nor will the Italian import grocer's stock it. The people in Italy will not buy it."

"Giancarlo, I can only hope you are right."

*****

The next day, I called Evan to set up a meeting with our distributor Sam Marzullo to discuss the sale of the business and Evan's new role. The following week we had lunch with Sam in LA. I explained to him that I had reached that point in my life to retire and briefly shared my opinion about *time*. I purposely introduced the discussion for Evan's benefit. "Sam, Evan will be taking on a new role as president of the US operation overseeing the distribution of our oil and working closely with all our distributors. However, he will still be working closely with your purveyors along with an assistant."

"I completely understand, Giancarlo, but I am concerned about my reorders this year. I need a plan from you considering the shortage. Have you arrived at a solution?"

"Sam, right now I can't answer that question. I am sure we will find a way to satisfy your needs."

After the meeting, I told Evan to arrange meetings with the rest of the distributors across the country.

For relaxation, Gina and I went to town to shop for books and music. We bought *A Raisin in the Sun* by Lorraine Hansberry.

We bought several new record albums: "Mack the Knife" by Bobby Darin and his "Dream Lover," "Kansas City" by Wilbert Harrison, and "Charlie Brown" by the Coasters. White singers were fast joining the rock and roll world. Even stars like Frank Sinatra changed their styles. He began working with black musicians like

Count Basie and singers Ella Fitzgerald, and Sammy Davis Jr. Slowly, the color barriers were being shattered.

February

Sam Marzullo invited us, the Venegonis, and Bomarittos on his yacht to celebrate my fifty-ninth birthday. The dinner on board was catered, and Sam spared no expense. The food and wine were superb. Sam toasted me and Gina, wishing us a happy retirement, and he led the group in singing "Happy Birthday." We watched the sunset, and my thoughts drew me back to San Remo. It was time.

At home, I had briefly stopped listening to TV news and even stopped delivery of the newspaper for a while, but Gina overruled me and restarted the newspaper. TV was addictive, and when I returned to the news, it was mainly because our commercials had started airing.

President Eisenhower addressed the nation and spoke about the US space program in reaction to the Russian Sputnik circling the globe. He announced the appointment of James Killian, the president of Massachusetts Institute of Technology as the head of the US space program. Eisenhower had been urged to take the program's control from the military and to put it in the hands of civilians.

A new organization was formed called NASA (National Aeronautics Space Administration) to handle the space program. It took over the divisions that were operating independently and scattered in different locations. The research facility in Langley, Virginia; the Ames Research Center in California; and the Vanguard missile satellite group operated by the navy all came under the aegis of the newly appointed administration.

In other news, the US Army invaded Lebanon in an overt intervention, another move by the president to exercise his doctrine to protect Middle Eastern countries where a threat of communism existed, thus putting the country at risk for another war. I told Gina that Eisenhower was fast pushing me to exit the Republican Party.

March

The weather was not cooperating with our desires to play golf and tennis. Cold, rainy days and strong winds prevailed throughout the month. There was no escape. The entire West Coast was plagued. It was named El Niño, and the heavy rains were causing flooding, erosion, and landslides along the California coast. In the Sierra and Rockies, heavy snows ruined the ski industry. The weather bureau had no way to forecast the future. Gina and I decided to depart early for Lucca.

Lucca
April

Our flight from Rome to Firenze was flawless, and as we stepped from the plane, we were greeted by the spring sun and calm weather, justifying our escape from El Niño. Salvatore greeted us with an ear-to-ear smile, a contrast from the last time we saw him, the relief from the fake olive oil no doubt being the cause.

We decided to have lunch and went to Cantinetta dei Verrazzano for focaccia and the delicious salami from Parma. It was good to be back in Tuscany.

The drive through Lucca was picturesque as always. The poppies had an early start and blanketed the landscape. Gina commented on it, and Salvatore related that it was due to the extra hot spring they were having.

At Gina's urging, I called Accardi Soap Manufacturing and La vie en Rose Cosmetics in Milan to set up appointments the following week. In addition, I set up a lunch meeting with Don Giovanni Ruggerri, our distributor.

Time to enjoy our stay dominated my mind. I asked Gina to plan a side trip along the coast in the ensuing weeks. She replied, "I would like to visit El Pelicano, an all-inclusive resort in Porto Ercole. It's on the West Coast on the Tyrrhenian Sea. I read about it in the *Town & Country* magazine. It's expensive, Giancarlo."

I reached in my pocket and pulled out a dollar bill and said nothing. She shook her head and said, "Got it."

We checked in to the Hotel Gallia in Milan. We didn't unpack. Gina had made reservations to see Leonardo da Vinci's *L'Ultima Cena* (*The Last Supper*). As we entered the room that displayed da Vinci's historical masterpiece, a small black-and-white photo was posted at the entrance. A wall with a fresco painted on it was featured, surrounded by rubble of what had been a building. We turned to our right. We saw *The Last Supper*, da Vinci's sixteenth-century marvel. We learned prior to painting the fresco, he spent three years on sketches and studies of Jesus and the apostles.

At the other end of the room stood the wall depicted in the photo. It was the *Crucifixion*, painted by Giovanni Donato at a church in Milan. During World War II, Allied bombers accidentally bombed the church, totally destroying it and leaving only the single wall with Donato's great work of art.

It was breathtaking. We were shocked at the size of *The Last Supper*, which is fifteen by thirty feet. To our right stood Thursday night's Passover dinner, on our left, Friday afternoon's crucifixion—surely one of life's never-to-be-forgotten experiences.

Again, *time* shook my memory. As often as we had been in Milan, we never had taken the time to visit this memorable site.

We had dinner at Antica Osteria Cavallini. The menu told a brief history of the restaurant. It had been in the same family since the early '30s. While we were perusing the menu, a waiter approached with a small plate on which he poured some olive oil from a bottle. We looked at him and smiled. I could not help myself and informed him it was our oil.

The next morning, we met with the Accardi Soap representatives. Gina started to relate the history of ancient European and Middle Eastern people's use of olive oil in soap. The marketing reps smiled when she finished. A box with no marking on it sat on the table. My intuition had told me when we sat that it contained a surprise. The lead person, Mr. Valore, took the lid off the box and put four different soaps in front of us. Two had lightly perfumed fragrances. The other two bore masculine fragrances.

What was really refreshing was the packaging. The background color was that of a ripe olive, and a small olive branch was in the background. The brand name was printed in black.

Gina asked if she could open them, and Mr. Valore said, "Signora, they are yours. Please feel free to open them. We also have a box to take with you."

I asked, "Signore Valore, when will you start marketing the soaps?"

He replied, "Signore Giambrone, when can you begin supplying us?"

I hesitated for a moment. "Signore, when do you need the oil and what kind of quantities will you be requiring?"

"We are starting to take test orders this coming week here in Milan and are promising delivery in September."

I responded, "That will be about the time we'll be harvesting next season's press, and delivery will be no problem."

During the exchange, Gina had opened the two soaps aimed for women and expressed her pleasure with them.

As we drove away, Gina said, "Well, Giancarlo, I guess we can say it was well worth the time we spent getting them to make the soap."

I smiled. Once again, the four-letter word surfaced.

Our next visit was with the La vie en Rose cosmetic group. They greeted us warmly, and on the conference table were several jars and packaged items, also two plates with pastries. They made espressos for us and served the pastry.

The lead scientist, Carmelo Marcelli, initiated the conversation with precise details about the first cosmetic, a moisturizer. Next was a body lotion and the third a shampoo with a built-in moisturizer. All contained the olive oil that we had left them on our previous visits. Gina said, "Signore Marcelli, we are overwhelmed. Are these for us to take?"

He replied, "Si, signora, with our compliments."

"Thank you, Signore Marcelli. When will you commence marketing these items?"

"As soon as you can begin shipping, Giancarlo. We are ready. We have made samples for our salesmen, and they are anxiously waiting for them. The semiannual fair here in Milan is next week. We are thinking of launching the first of November in time for the Christmas holiday season."

"There will be no trouble shipping to you in early October, signore. Please get me an estimate of your needs no later than September 1."

We agreed to the target dates and departed.

We had a nice visit with Don Giovani Ruggeri and received warm compliments about Salvatore, and we drove back to Lucca, satisfied with the achievements of the past two days. Thanks to Gina's efforts, the olive oil business was taking on a whole new life.

CHAPTER 19

May

We drove to El Pelicano. The drive through Tuscany along the Tyrrhenian Sea was like a movie travelogue. The sea was so smooth, it looked like you could walk on it.

On arrival at the hotel, the concierge took us on a brief tour. There were two beautiful restaurants, the first for breakfast and lunch, the other exclusively for dinner, each with a magnificent view of the sea. She showed us the spa and beauty salon, with an area for men's services, and next to it, a full-blown gym.

She then escorted us to our suite. The walk-in closet was the size of a small hotel room, as was the bathroom, which included a separate shower large enough for six people. The balcony had two chaise lounges and a small dining table with a bottle of prosecco on ice. The main room was den-like with lounge chairs and a TV and a small portable refrigerator stocked with beer, soda, and various treats.

We left with the concierge and headed to lunch. The menu featured many fresh seafood dishes, and several house-made pastas. We made our selections, and I ordered a carafe of white wine. We had dessert with a flan-like custard that satisfied our sweet tooth. Afterward, Gina suggested we walk off the meal at the beach.

The mild surf from the sea rinsed our feet. It was like bath water. Our minds were somewhere else. We were not speaking for a good twenty minutes, and I broke the ice. "Gina, you're being very pensive. Where are you right now?"

"Many places, Giancarlo, somewhat sad. I was thinking how different our life would have been if our baby had lived. I thought about my early childhood, school friends, and wondered what hap-

173

pened to a few of my girlfriends and a couple of boys I had crushes on." A tear dropped.

Then you entered the picture. I thought about the day you hired me in 1942 and falling in love with you. It seems like yesterday, and here we are in the final year of the '50s.

By the way, you, too, have been silent. What were you thinking?"

I hesitated to answer. I, too, had often reflected back to the sad day when we lost the baby. It was indelible in my mind. My thoughts were even deeper. There is no question we would have had at least one more child had the baby lived, which would have dramatically changed our lifestyle.

"I was conscious of your mind being somewhere else, and I didn't want to interrupt, so I decided to enjoy the moment, and this time together away from the olive-oil business."

I thought, *There is that four-letter word again.*

I put my arm around her, sharing her pain about the baby. I held her tightly and said nothing. There were no words in my vocabulary to ease her pain. I knew the minute I tried to console her would bring tears.

The week at El Pelicano was joyous. The food and service topped anything we had ever experienced at any other resort. We returned to the sea and walked the beach a second time, and the daily sunsets with a glass of wine from our balcony left us with memories to savor for a long time.

Siracusa
July

I began reading *A Raisin in the Sun*, written by a black woman, Lorraine Hansberry. I told Gina I had no recollection of a black woman writer having a best-selling book on the *New York Times*. The book begins in the early '40s in an apartment occupied by a black family on the south side of Chicago.

The theme centers on two things: dreams that vary between the children and the racial discrimination they were experiencing. She pushed them to follow their dreams. The eldest daughter dreams of being a doctor so that she can dedicate her life to cure people. The son dreams of achieving wealth so that he can provide the family lifestyle of the rich and famous. One of the mother's dreams was to escape the crime-ridden squalor of their neighborhood.

As the children age, their dreams fade, but the mother, through hard work and savings, achieves her dream. They buy a house in an all-white neighborhood. Shortly after moving in, they are approached by a man who offers to buy the house with a substantial profit. They refuse the offer, taking a stand against the racism, thus asserting pride versus becoming victims of desperation.

The mother gathers them and says, "What happens when you allow dreams to fail to become reality? They dry up like raisins." A beautifully written story showing the crush of racism on a family.

*****

I continued to be disturbed by the news about US involvement in Vietnam. I was not alone. The divide among American people continued to grow. A report by a New York journalist, Albert Colegrove, surfaced about the main goal of North Vietnam to destroy the South Vietnam government. The report was published as a series of articles exposing the corruption in the Diệm government and the scandalous waste of money. It prompted an investigation by the State Department, but the lobbyists in DC denounced it, and it was overturned through pressure from Congress, led by powerful senator William Fulbright.

I followed the entire process, and could not believe how naive our country had become. Eisenhower, who campaigned in 1952 on keeping the country out of war, had reneged on his promise. We had more than a thousand so-called American military advisors in South Vietnam.

August

I received a cable from Salvatore. He and Giuseppe had met with all the distributors in Italy and explained the sale of the business and that he and his brother would be taking it over. In addition, Giuseppe would be relocating to Bologna after the harvest in early October. He also was pleased to report a bumper crop of olives would soon be harvested and projected the yield would surpass last year's production

I cabled back and thanked him for the news and informed him to expect orders from the soap and cosmetic firms in Milan. I advised him to be sure to contact those firms on his next trip to Milan.

At breakfast, I let Gina read both cables. She was delighted and said, "So Giancarlo, this sounds like you should be able to wrap up the sale when we return to Palm Springs."

"True Gina. I am as anxious as you are. I am ready for the next part of our life together. The past eight years have been both challenging and rewarding. I am proud of the fact we saved my family's historic business, but we paid a price in doing so. It was that precious four-letter word. Money, pride, and success can't buy time. There is no price."

Palm Springs
October

We called for a rendezvous with our friends the day we arrived. We invited them for a barbecue at our house Saturday evening. After dinner, Tom Venegoni asked about the sale of the business, and I replied it would be completed after the first of the year. Sharon asked, "So what are your plans once it is completed, Giancarlo?"

I said, "Ask the lady sitting next to me. It's her call, Sharon."

Gina said, "We have no set plans. However, Mr. Giambrone turns sixty in February. What do you people think of celebrating the big one at a great resort in Italy. We recently discovered two incredible slices of heaven, both on the beautiful Tyrrhenian Sea. San Remo on the Northern Italian Riviera and a resort called El Pelicano a short drive from our house in Lucca."

Sandra said, "I have an idea. Why not spend a week at each of them?"

Tom looked around the room and said, "Well, gentlemen, it looks like the ladies have made the decision for our 1960 vacations."

Tony said, "Isn't that the way it always is? I second Sandra's motion. What do you have to say, Giancarlo?"

"As I said earlier, just ask the lady sitting next to me."

We all laughed.

November

We all went to see the movie *Ben-Hur*. It was the most expensive movie ever made to date. It cost $15 million to produce it. It was a massive undertaking. This was a remake of the original in 1925. William Wyler directed it, and the cast consisted of Hollywood's elite. It was set in Judea in AD 26. Charlton Heston played the lead as Judah Ben-Hur. The rest of the cast included British actor Jack Hawkins, Stephen Boyd, Hugh Griffith, Haya Harareet, Cathy O'Donnell, and Sam Jaffe.

Judah refuses Roman authority and is enslaved and ends up in the galley of a ship for three years owned by a wealthy Roman. While at sea, a severe storm destroys the ship, and Judah saves the life of the owner and slave master. He appeals to the emperor Tiberius to free Judah from slavery and is granted, and he adopts him as his son.

Judah is offered an opportunity to become a gladiator and refuses. He becomes an expert charioteer. Later, he enters a race against the man who subjected him to slavery and defeats him in a contested race. Sandwiched in between all this is his life as a free man and his love life.

Was the movie worth the $15-million cost? Hard to say.

December

I set up a meeting with our attorney Ben Silverstein for early January. I asked that he form a new corporation called the Lucca Olive Oil Company of North America, naming Evan Severino president, Nancy Garrett as secretary, and Brock Severino as vice president of marketing. I sent a similar cable to our council in Lucca to do the same, naming Salvatore as chief operating officer and Giuseppe as VP of marketing.

We spent the holidays in Laguna Beach with Sandra and Tom and visited for lunch and dinner with Sharon and Tony. The year 1959 ended as it had begun—*time* with the people we loved. I was looking forward to the coming year, a year of closure.

CHAPTER 20

Palm Springs
January 1960

The morning newspaper on January 2 woke the country with the announcement that John Fitzgerald Kennedy, the junior senator from Massachusetts, was seeking the Democratic nomination for president. He had earlier written *Profiles in Courage*, winning the Pulitzer Prize that brought him national recognition.

He was a World War II hero, the son of Joe Kennedy, the former ambassador to England and grandson of John "Honey Fitz," long-time Democratic politician, who had served two terms as mayor of Boston. The young contender could change the face of political leadership in the US. The senator had it all. He was handsome, well educated, has command of the English language, a gifted speaker, and he was married to one of the most attractive, well-educated women in America.

I was eager to move on with the transfer of the business. I met Evan, Nancy, and Brock with Jimmy Boscamp at Bank of America. They signed the documents for the line of credit for the new company. Jimmy spoke highly about his early days working with me in Chicago. It was somewhat embarrassing. He praised me for giving him his start in the banking business.

I put it down, turning the praise to him for his dedication, hard work, and integrity. We used his conference room and signed the legal documents, completing the sale. This was phase 1 of the sale.

Then the three of us went to lunch at Tony's and celebrated. I took a few minutes to reflect on our meeting and spoke of my pride in their development. These three young kids right out of college had become top businesspeople in a short period of time. Jimmy Boscamp's kind words echoed in my mind, and self-satisfaction climaxed my thoughts. It was well worth the *time* spent grooming them.

I had mixed emotions on the drive back to Palm Springs. I had just put my baby up for adoption. I recalled how boredom had crept into my life in 1950, when Giuseppe's death rescue arrived. Now it was *time* to move on.

Gina and I went to the club for lunch, and I shared the previous day's events, along with the emotional feelings I encountered. She said, "Giancarlo, get serious. You'll be sixty in a few days. You're the one who said, "It's no longer fun."

Rest assured I will not allow you to get bored. You'll now have time to play golf and tennis with no business on your mind, no planes to jump on, no pressure. We can spend more time together and with our friends. You'll be able to read those books we recently purchased. There's four of them sitting on the shelf that need your attention."

"Thanks, Gina. You're right. It's just hard to turn it off. I experienced it when I sold the banks and the same downtime when we sold the buildings in the late '40s."

When we got home I buried myself in the newspaper. The economy was the big news. The recession was slowing due to major exports to Japan and Europe. Unemployment dropped mainly due to the resurgence of auto sales and construction.

March

The warm spring weather gave us time to enjoy the freedom from the olive oil business, and golf and tennis took up a good part of our time. The TV networks began broadcasting great movies of the past. We watched *Casablanca* with Ingrid Bergman and Humphrey Bogart, 1941's Academy Award winner.

We went into town and met Sharon and Tony for lunch to discuss our future trip to Italy and to celebrate my sixtieth birthday. The plan was to meet in Rome with Sandra and Tom for a few days and then hire a driver to take us to El Pelicano for a week and travel from there to San Remo for the second week.

We met our travel agent and booked the trip. Our plan included two nights in Rome, staying at Hotel d'Inghilterra Roma. We booked a guide for the two days and also made reservations for dinner at La Campana, the oldest restaurant in Rome dating back to the sixteenth century, and La Carbonara.

Before heading home, we stopped to buy a few of *Billboard's* top-ten records—Lloyd Price's "Stagger Lee," Dinah Washington's "What a Diff'rence a Day Made," Nina Simone's "I Love You, Porgy," and Ray Charles's "What'd I Say." On the drive home, Gina said, "Do you know that all the singers on every record we bought are black. This decade has had a major impact in music for black entertainers.

Rome
April

The six of us checked in to the Hotel d'Inghilterra. Gina and I had been there, but it was a first for the Venegonis and Bomarittos. The meeting with our guide to see the Colosseum was at 2:00 p.m., and we didn't have time to unpack. Hunger and jet lag got the better of us, but we managed to arrive on time. Our guide recognized Gina and me and greeted us with hugs.

She did a great job on the history of the epic Roman treasure. For the first time, Gina and I learned about the bronze statue outside the Colosseum on the way to the forum. She told the story of how the maniacal Nero had it made in an image of himself, and it was deemed the Colossus of Nero and originally placed in his palace. Later, it was moved to its current location, thus the name of the building where it stands.

We had dinner at La Campana, the oldest ristorante in Rome, opened in the same location in 1518. Tony was beside himself and voiced shock when he learned the date. "I can't imagine how any business could exist after that many years and remain in the same location."

We all agreed. The food highlighted the entire day. It was colossal.

The next morning, we met our guide at the Vatican, and again, her knowledge of Michelangelo's magnificent work made a lasting impression on our guests.

As we walked to St. Peter's Basilica, Sandra said, "Only in Italy can one see two of the world's ancient sites dating back centuries and in a restaurant that dates with them. Can you imagine the possibility of Michelangelo having dinner at La Campana after a hard day painting the ceiling at the Vatican?"

Gina and I learned another lesson once inside St. Peter's. Our first stop was the altar with Michelangelo's famous sculpture of the *Pietà*, Mary holding Jesus in her arms after the Crucifixion. He was twenty-three years old when he created it between 1498 and 1499. His penchant for detail depicted Mary's grief and love for her son.

Later, it was Sandra who remarked, "I am overwhelmed. In a short three hours for a few pennies, we have seen two masterpieces of perhaps the greatest artist in history, both dating back five centuries within walking distance of each other. I am disappointed we only have two days in this eternal city." It was an epic visit.

We had dinner at La Carbonara that night, founded in 1912. It was the first time for Gina and me. Gina read about it in *Town & Country* magazine, and it lived up to its reputation. The food and service were incredible.

The next morning, we went to the Borghese Gardens museum. The museum contained some of Italy's finest works of art, the most important being Gian Lorenzo Bernini's brilliant lifelike sculpture of the mythological god Apollo and Daphne the nymph. Gina explained the story behind the sculpture to the group. Apollo sought the virgin Daphne, and she continued to rebuff him. He was relentless, and she finally appealed to her father, also a god, and he turned her into a tree. Our friends were speechless staring at Bernini's seventeenth-century masterpiece.

After lunch, we departed for El Pelicano. The drive along the Tyrrhenian Sea was marvelous, and our friends were ecstatic at the scenery. The warm spring sunshine welcomed us to Tuscany. After we checked in to the hotel, the concierge showed us around and informed us she had reserved a table for dinner at the seven-o'clock seating.

We had lunch on the beach and later took a leisurely walk in the sand. This was far removed from the hectic pace of the previous days in Rome. The salty breeze from the sea was refreshing. Dinner was as expected. Two bottles of wine were a compliment from the concierge, and our friends expressed gratitude to us for bringing them to our hidden gem.

The ensuing days of perfect weather, great food and wine, having cocktails together, and watching sunsets concluded the first week. The entire drive to San Remo was along the sea. We stopped in Forte dei Marmi for lunch and arrived in San Remo midafternoon. The week seemed to be on a fast train. The days were somewhat of a blur. Thanks to beautiful, balmy days, we relaxed, ate great food, played tennis, and enjoyed our time together.

On our last day, Sharon said, "Gina and Giancarlo, this is sad. In a couple of days, we will be heading our separate ways, and we will not see you for nine months."

We were not looking forward to their departure. We had our final dinner on the balcony in our suite. Gina had a cake with a single candle brought in, and the group sang "Happy Birthday." I thought about Sharon's comment. It was a sad moment. Tony toasted me, we clicked glasses, and I thanked everyone for making my sixtieth one of the best ever.

We drove to Lucca the next day, and our guests spent the weekend. Anna was in heaven cooking for six hungry people, receiving kudos after every meal. Sharon and Tony headed east to Firenze for a few days, while Tom and Sandra headed north to Milan. We had shared our experience seeing *The Last Supper* with them.

*****

May

I called to set up a meeting with our account executive Lorenzo Paneri at Banca Monte dei Paschi in Milan. I told him about the sale of the business to Salvatore and Giuseppe. We had been doing business with the bank since the '30s.

Lorenzo welcomed us warmly. He was acquainted with Salvatore because they dealt with one another, but he had not meant Giuseppe. Lorenzo knew our business well, and the meeting was more of a formality. I did ask for a small line of credit, and it was easily granted.

We presented the documents regarding the new company, and Lorenzo graciously invited us to lunch in the bank's dining room. Thus, the final page on the sale of the business was complete. I was comforted by the fact that the business would be in good hands.

Bernini's Apollo and Daphene

Michelangelo's Pieta

CHAPTER 21

Siracusa
June

The trip to our summer home was especially pleasant. I felt like a giant building had been lifted from my shoulders. Gina asked, "So, Giancarlo, how do you feel now that the business is sold? Any remorse?"

"Funny you should ask. Knowing that in Italy, there basically is no change—the same people at every level will be running the show, with similar circumstances prevailing in the States—I am comfortable, much more so than if we had sold to a strange firm. They undoubtedly would have made changes. It is a textbook example of what companies do when they buy a company.

This is especially true when a public company is the buyer. They have to report earnings to Wall Street, and they begin cutting overhead wherever they can. The chief financial officer gets involved and usually replaces many of the people that brought the company to the dance. In time, like a slow cancer, the company no longer resembles its old self. I am confident none of that will happen. Lucca Olive Oil is in good hands."

In the newspaper, I read that at the Democratic convention John Fitzgerald Kennedy defeated Sen. Lyndon Baines Johnson and won the nomination for president. Kennedy named Johnson his running mate. Vice President Richard Nixon was his opponent representing the Republican Party, and he had an early lead at the polls. Kennedy challenged Nixon to a series of TV debates, and the battle for the November election was on.

I was sick of the news and stopped watching TV. Gina was on me about my never-ending battle with news makers. "I don't understand why you can't just watch them and deal with it. Good or bad, there's nothing you can do to change it."

I smiled.

It was time to settle in and enjoy our time in this beautiful part of the world. We went to the sea and walked the beach. We had lunch at a little trattoria, shared a carafe of wine, and allowed time to take charge—no news, no business, no aggravation.

Gina went to town to shop for a few things for Alena. She bought the *Herald-Tribune* and left it on my desk but didn't tell me. Later, I went to make a call and saw it. I did not acknowledge it. Later, I brought it to the patio when we sat for lunch. She ignored me. After lunch, I picked it up and began reading, and we both started laughing.

The news told of John Kennedy's civil rights speech. Without question, he was catering to black Americans, a typical political appeal to get their vote. It was not timed well because black Civil Rights leader Medgar Evers was assassinated shortly thereafter.

Meanwhile, Fidel Castro and his communist-controlled regime in Cuba made world news by nationalizing three US banks. I put the news aside to enjoy the day.

We were blessed with the weather. The sun was hidden at times by picturesque clouds, and a light breeze kept things cool. I began reading author Harper Lee's controversial novel *To Kill a Mockingbird*. It topped the *New York Times*'s bestseller list. The author grew up in a small town in Alabama, was well educated, and personally observed racial injustice in the early 1930s. She was incensed at the bus incident that took place in Montgomery, Alabama. She drew on a historical trial of a black man who had been accused of the rape of a white woman.

The plot introduces a white liberal attorney who stands up for bigotry, insisting a black man deserves to be treated as an equal citizen under the law. He proceeds to defend a black man who has been arrested for raping a white woman—a great novel showing the injustices in our country.

My attitude about taking *time* remained indelible in my mind. After dinner, I asked Gina if she was interested in taking a trip to Spain. She looked at and said, "Mr. Giambrone, we just spent three weeks earlier this year on a vacation with our friends. Please don't tell me you are already getting bored. Let's go see a movie, *Spartacus* with Kirk Douglas."

I smiled. "I am a little bored, but rest assured business is far from my mind. What's the movie about?"

"It takes place in early Roman days, and actress Jean Simmons has a prominent role."

Spartacus was everything the movie critics said it was, an epic movie based on the somewhat-true story of early Rome. Spartacus, a slave, refuses to adhere to certain demands by his slave master. It begins in the first century BC in Rome. Spartacus is sentenced to die from starvation and is rescued by a wealthy Roman who buys his freedom. He is sent to gladiator school and joins other slaves. He is frequented by a female slave played by Jean Simmons but refuses to sleep with her. They become friends.

Spartacus escapes and recruits a large group of fugitives and attacks Rome at various locations and is captured. He is forced to fight another gladiator and kills the opponent. Meanwhile, a love story is intertwined, and he marries (Jean Simmons) and has a child with the mistress. His goal was to free Rome from slavery. It sounded like a movie I wanted to see.

September

We celebrated Gina's birthday with a return trip to Ragusa. We had dinner at the little restaurant where we dined on our first trip. The owner remembered us and brought a plate of house-made ravioli to our table, along with a second plate on which he poured olive oil it. We both smiled. I handed him a note when I went to the washroom, stating it was her birthday.

After dinner, he and the crew brought a small cake and sang "Happy Birthday" in Italian to her. A smile and a single tear fell. A familiar thought crossed my mind: *time.*

October

The *Herald-Tribune* reported the arrival of the long-awaited expanded color-TV programs. At the same time, Martin Luther King was arrested for a sit-in at a restaurant. He was quickly tried and convicted and sentenced to four months in prison. Robert and John Kennedy appealed to the judge in the case, and he was released. JFK took the time to call his wife, Coretta, and gave her the news. The press played it as a political move.

November

Kennedy was making strategic moves in the states Eisenhower won in the previous election. He carefully avoided critiquing the president, a smart move because the nation as a whole liked "Ike." Meanwhile, Lyndon Johnson was following the same pattern, traveling in the South, which was his stronghold. Frank Sinatra came out for JFK early and began his move with the Hollywood crowd.

Nixon's lead in the polls began sliding as the first TV debate approached. In that debate, JFK's strength prevailed. He was a great speaker. Nixon had suffered from a virus, and Kennedy won the debate. The next day, the polls showed his small deficit moved to a small lead. But Nixon recovered and won the next two. The third was deemed a draw. The polls had it so close, there was no favorite to win. Sixty-six million people watched those debates.

After the polls closed on Election Day, the ballot counting continued into the early-morning hours, and Kennedy won by one of the smallest margins in history and became the thirty-fifth president of the US. This was young, new leadership for our country.

Los Angeles

Sharon and Tony greeted us on our return to LA. We drove to Tony's restaurant for dinner, and Sandra and Tom surprised us. We exchanged hugs and celebrated our return with our cherished friends. After dinner Tony startled the group. "Well, Giancarlo, I have decided to join you and Tom in the unemployment line. We have accepted an offer for our restaurant."

After the initial shock, Tom said, "Well, Tony, I am not attempting to minimize your announcement. Sandra and I recently bought a town house in the desert. Looks like we are going to be playing a lot of golf and tennis."

Gina was next. "This clan is getting tighter. We need someone's birthday to celebrate next spring's vacation together. Is anyone interested in Spain? My husband has put in a request."

Sharon was first to raise her hand. "We are in!"

Sandra simultaneously said, "We are too."

Tom, Tony, and I just stared at the three women and laughed.

It was our turn to host the Christmas and New Year holidays. Gina did her usual Italian dinner for Christmas Eve. Tony supplied the wine, and Sandra made cannoli. We had dinner for New Year's Eve catered by the country club. We tried to stay awake and watch the ball drop in Times Square, but the food and wine got the best of us.

When I woke up the next morning, there were bodies everywhere. Tony and Sharon were asleep on the living room couches. Sandra was sleeping on a chaise lounge in the den. Tom was snuggled next to her. My bride was asleep in another world.

I made coffee and found an empty chair. It was hard to believe it was 1961. Again, my mind centered on the four-letter word. It took me back to April 1950 in Antibes, celebrating my fiftieth. Giuseppe Fragale's death and the impact it had on our life surfaced. Next, the intensity of the olive oil business and the eight years it consumed.

I wondered what decision I would have made had I known I'd be spending eight years to build the business. Then my father's advice came into focus: "Don't look back, Giancarlo. You can't change the past and never waste *time* looking forward. Take life one day at a time."

My reverie was interrupted when Gina approached and grabbed me. "Happy New Year, handsome. I love you."

It was 1960, and ten years faded in the morning sunrise. It was time to wake our friends and welcome 1961. I had no idea what lay waiting for Gina and me in the future.

A happy life consists of tranquility of mind.

—Cicero

The End

ABOUT THE AUTHOR

Meet Joe Reina, entrepreneurial businessman turned author. Joe came up through the ranks in the apparel industry from salesman to manager, store owner, business mogul, and real-estate developer. An avid reader of history, he took the lessons from the past to navigate the economic ups and downs of the midtwentieth century. His businesses entailed international travel and enabled him to explore a good part of the world. That exposure helped satisfy his lifelong desire to experience the pleasure of meeting people worldwide and then sharing his travels with his family and friends.

Throughout his successes, Joe never forgot his roots of growing up on the Hill in St. Louis and the fortitude of his spirited mother, an émigré from Sicily. He wrote the book *The Goat Sleeps in the Kitchen* to tell her remarkable story of becoming a successful businesswoman in the early twentieth century. His fascination with that era resulted in the birth of his fictional alter ego, Giancarlo Giambrone, one of the world's great entrepreneurs. Now comes the sequel to Giancarlo Giambrone, *The Golden Age*.

Joe lives in Scottsdale, Arizona.